First published in 2004
jointly by

Gracewing
2 Southern Avenue
Leominster
Herefordshire HR6 0QF

Nova Millennium Romae
1 Largo Angelicum
00184 Roma
Italy

ISBN 0-85244-665-9

Translated by Brian Williams

By kind permission of the Edizioni Studium - Roma
First Italian Edition published 1993

Printed by Rotostampa Group S.r.l.
Via Tiberio Imperatore, 23 - 00145 Roma

Mario D'Addio

THE GALILEO CASE

Trial / Science / Truth

Contents

PREFACE

The present work, which first appeared in the "Rivista di storia della Chiesa in Italia", Considerazioni sui processi di Galileo, 1983, No. 1, pp. 1-52; 1984, No. 1, pp. 47-114, and in the "Quaderni" of the same Review, has a different title in this new edition: The Galileo Case: Trial / Science / Truth, *which seems to be more appropriate to the essential aspects of the Galileo affair. Some slight changes of a formal character have been made in certain points, and it has been thought appropriate to expand the enquiry into the Galileo question in the seventeenth century in order to give more precise details of the precedents of the decision by the Holy Office in August 1820, which in effect annulled the judgment of 1633. Account has also been taken of the further bibliography which appeared between 1984 and 1992.*

The writer has had the opportunity to take a close interest in Galileo in the course of his studies in the Italian seventeenth century – in particular on Campanella and the German humanist Gaspare Scioppio, friends, supporters and correspondents of the Pisan scientist – and in his work on the Pontifical Commission for the study of the Galileo question. The reconstruction of the complex events of Galileo's case, which centres on the two trials of 1616 and 1633, is based on the historical sources: above all on the records of the trial and the correspondence published by Favaro, as well as on the writings of Galileo which refer to the theory of heliocentricity and those of his opponents, in the light of the already well-established results of historical enquiry. Special attention has been paid to the history of science, with the aim of providing greater clarity about the terms of the dispute between advocates and opponents of the Copernican thesis. The criterion followed in the historical reconstruction of the Galileo trials is that of bringing the reader "into direct contact" with the documents, the opinions and the judgments of those who played an important part in the two trials, with the aim of providing a complete historical portrait of the Galileo question.

The two trials are intimately connected with the very interesting scientific, theological-philosophical and exegetical debate between Galileo, his friends and disciples, and his opponents, which involved the whole of Italian secular and ecclesiastical thought in the first three decades of the seventeenth century, and which then took on a European dimension. Both the former and the latter were searching for truth, which when it is presented as a radical innovation of traditional knowledge is difficult to "prove" and thus equally difficult to understand. Hence the feeling of substantial uncertainty, a hesitancy between yes and no which transpires in the ecclesiastical circles most directly involved in the Galileo question, which inspired the caution, the reservations, the perplexities with regard to a sentence of condemnation. These hesitations can be found in both 1616 and 1633.

We should remind the reader that the conclusions of the work of the Commission were formulated by Cardinal Paul Poupard on the occasion of the papal audience to the members of the Pontifical Academy of Sciences (31st November 1992), in which Pope John Paul II specified the motives why "the painful misunderstanding of the presumed opposition involved between science and faith now belongs to the past".

The first edition of the book carried a presentation by Cardinal Gabriel Marie Garrone, coordinator of the commission, which it seems appropriate to include at the conclusion of this brief introductory note.

Le Saint-Père dans son Discours à l'Académie Pontificale des Sciences le 10 novembre 1979, s'inscrivant d'une manière décisive dans la ligne ouverte par le deuxième Concile du Vatican, a entendu lever l'hypothèque qui pèse sur le problème du Procès de Galilée. D'une part, l'exploitation partisane n'avait pas manqué bien souvent autour de cette question, mais, d'autre part, il était difficile de contester qu'un certain souci apologétique ait pu inspirer, et même légitimer, quelque défiance. C'est pourquoi le Pape décidait de confier à une groupe de personnalités qualifiées dans les secteurs divers intéressés à cette affaire, la mission de donner à son vœu une première réalisation. La Commission prévue comportait une section exégétique, une section scientifique e épistémologique, et une section d'histoire.

La section d'histoire a été confiée à la direction de Mons. Michele Maccarrone, Président du Comité Pontifical des sciences historiques, qui a chargé le Prof. Mario d'Addio de l'Université de Rome, membre de la Commission Pontificale d'Etudes Galiléiens de compiler une étude du Procès de Galilée.

Je suis heureux de présenter l'œuvre du Prof d'Addio qui est publiée dans les "Quaderni" de la "Rivista di storia della Chiesa in Italia".

CARDINAL GABRIEL MARIE GARRONE
Coordinateur du Groupe d'Etude
concernant l'affaire Galilée

SECTION 1

I. THE 1616 TRIAL

1. The historical problem of the Galileo issue

It is a well known fact that the trial of Galileo was the conclusion of a long, embittered disputation which in many respects was to occupy the minds of Italian educated, academic and ecclesiastical circles, especially those of Florence and Rome, between 1613 and 1633. Astronomy was a passion of the times, partly because it was closely connected with astrology, from which the powerful sought to shed light on their future. This meant that every discovery, every news-item which concerned the vault of the heavens, the stars, was received and commented on with the liveliest interest. This is enough to explain the widespread echo raised by Galileo's discoveries – the satellites of Jupiter, the surface of the Moon, the phases of Venus, the form of Saturn – and the first criticisms, the polemical observations by those who remained faithful to the Artistotelian concept of nature, and of the skies in particular, who could not admit the existence of celestial phenomena which threw doubt on or openly contradicted the Aristotelian-Ptolemaic cosmos, and hence the principles on which it was based: the first denunciation by the hotheaded, at times somewhat overheated, defenders of the theological and religious notion of the Ptolemaic system. And as is well known, this found its indubitable confirmation in certain famous passages in the Scriptures.

It was not only curiosity and scientific interest, anxiety over statements which could dissolve long-established religious convictions, but also the arcane, the mysterious, the marvellous and the grandiose, which the discoveries of Galileo seemed to be herding towards a new "mode of being in the world". In Italian learned circles in the first half of the seventeenth century there was a strong existential tension in which the need for the "new", for new ideas was expressed, in opposition to the desire, coming from a natural psychological reaction, to defend established truths based on a consolidated tradition and on the evidence of common sense. The debate between "innovators" and "traditionalists" was characterised by the particular animus of a learned society, inclined to dispute in the academies and to meet up in a kind of "oratorical duel" which often aroused jealousies, scruples, one-sidedness, and the taste for putting one's opponent to rout.

None of the participants in the debate managed to rise above this logic of the "academic discourse". Galileo, the theorist of the experimental world and of modern science, was also a master of the art of "inventing" and "constructing" compelling arguments to prove his thesis and defeat his adversary.[1] We only have to recall the *Saggiatore*, a work which can certainly be described as the "prologue to all future natural science", but which at the same time carries on, in pages of high literary value, a "dialectic" of a purely humanistic type. As is well known, the thesis maintained and "proved" by Galileo - that a comet is a completely illusory astronomical phenomenon - is not true, while that sustained by his Jesuit adversary - the comet is a celestial body - is true. It is from this that the complexity of the debate comes: motives of sentiment and personal issues merge in this debate with cultural, religious, philosophical and, of course, purely scientific interests, which concerned Galileo as they did many of his adversaries. It also arises from the fact that the old and the new were intimately connected in a dialectical relationship which must be kept in mind when any historical evaluation is made of the debate and its "judicial conclusions".

The verdict of June 1633, far from putting an end to the debate, as Urban VIII had hoped, had the effect of radicalising it. On the one hand, truth, on the other, error; on the one hand science, on the other, dogmatic and authoritarian religion. This confrontation was the implicit premise of the Galileo issue during the second half of the seventeenth century, and was assumed and explicitly understood by the ethos of the Enlightenment. For this epoch, the matter of Galileo acquired a symbolic value: the condemnation was, *a contrario*, an irrefutable proof of scientific reasoning. Hence the extremely lively interest in this question, and above all in the two processes which had been held under the seal of secrecy. Even a politician, general and statesman shared this interest, absorbed though he was by very different interests and governmental matters. Napoleon, on the occasion of the transfer of the Archive of the Inquisition to France, explicitly requested the acts of the trials of Galileo, with the pre-determined intention to publish them. Subsequent political events did not permit the realisation of this initiative; the codex containing the "proceedings of the trial" was not handed over on the occasion of the restitution of the archive to the Holy See. It remained in France, and was finally recovered by the Papacy only after long diplomatic negotiations, in 1843.[2]

Interest in the Galileo case was revived with the publication of the acts, and in the context of positivist philosophy and culture, the opposition between reason/science and religion was resumed. Naturally this gave historical research a declared ideological bias on the one side, and a specific spirit of apologetics on the other. Allowing for these limitations, a work of more profound critical research was begun, from the historical and, above all, the philological standpoint, with the publication of a number of important documents on Galileo,[3] and with a precise historical reconstruction of the cultural and scientific environment in which the case of Galileo took place. This also included the personalities involved in the case, and its most significant episodes, with careful enquiries into the history of science. This culminated later in the national edition of the works of Galileo, thanks to the truly admirable work of Antonio Favaro. On the basis of this wide, almost complete, documentation, the historical investigation over the last fifty years has been concentrating more and more specifically on the complex aspects of the Galileo question, researching not only into the Italian cultural context, but also into that of Europe as a whole, in its relationship to the renewal of scholarship brought about by the work of Copernicus, of Tycho Brahe and Kepler. This has made it much easier to understand the scientific arguments of Galileo and his opponents. The case of Galileo has thus little by little been placed in an historical context, considered more as an historical event, and thus to be studied historically. The former ideological viewpoints have been weakened, and certain defensive tones have been substantially abandoned. On the occasion of the third centenary of Galileo's death, Agostino Gemelli stated: "[...] Catholics do not fear to recognise genuinely that the process against him was an error [...] it was an error of the theologians which, as Pastor observed, has become a constant rebuke".[4]

The Copernicus/Galileo issue is in many ways the history of an "error", of the historically objective difficulties in the way of recognising the new scientific truth. The Copernican theory was condemned first of all because it was "false and absurd in philosophy", i.e. on the plane of reason, and then because it was contrary to Scripture. It would have meant, in the last analysis that if the thesis of Copernicus was accepted, it would have been necessary to deny the reason that was based on the common experience of our senses.

Burtt has stressed the extreme difficulty of abandoning this type of rationality: "One could say that even if there had not been any other religious scruple which was opposed to Copernican astronomy, sensible people all over Europe, and especially those who were gifted with the spirit of empiricism, would have considered it a foolish invitation to reap the premature fruits of an uncontrolled imagination, preferring it to safe inductions elaborated a little at a time. Since there is this stress on empiricism, which characterises the philosophy of the moment, it is worth remembering this fact. Contemporary empiricists, had they been living in the sixteenth century, would at first have ridiculed the new philosophy of the universe".[5]

The eleven theologians who expressed their opinion on the occasion of the trial of 1616 were certainly not greatly adept in the complex questions of astronomy and mathematics, but they were not the only ones to judge the Copernican hypothesis in that way. Only a short time later, their opinion was to be confirmed by a philosopher who is justly recognised as one of the fathers of the experimental method and a forerunner of the enlightenment, Francis Bacon. In his *Novum Organum*, he placed the Copernican system among the "idola tribus" of which truly rational men should rid themselves: an "invention", conceived solely in order to "overturn" the mathematical calculations of the planet: a completely fictitious astronomic system, based on the movement of the earth; a real absurdity which was founded on abstract mathematical hypotheses, and which he did not hesitate to judge as "utterly false".[6]

At the outset, the truth, which opens new horizons and radically renews our knowledge, is not an "experimental datum"; it is, rather, an intellectual vision, which anticipates all the data of experience and which imposes itself on the mind also, and in some ways above all, against the acquired and traditional "sensible experience". Galileo himself says so: "[…] Nor can I sufficiently admire the ingenuity of those who […] have by the vivacity of their intellect put such pressure on their own senses that they have been able to oppose what normal discourse dictated, what the sensible experiences showed them most clearly to the contrary".[7] But it is not enough to "see" the truth mentally, we must demonstrate it, and then communicate it to others so that in their turn they may be able to understand it. And this inevitably involves the use of terms and expressions that are sometimes inadequate to the task; hence the misunderstandings, the ambiguities, the errors. The truth, in order to be recognised, must be "verified". Error is the inevitable moment of "falsification" which, historically accompanies every announcement of the truth.

The whole affair of Galileo, at the level of both secular and clerical culture, was characterised by the error-truth experience: in this context the story of the two trials reveals the uncertainty, perplexity, doubt and reservation which characterise the attitudes of ecclesiastical circles and people in authority involved in the question. One gets the clear impression that within the Curia there was not a fixed orientation towards the traditional notions. The Curia was substantially divided between the supporters of Galileo and his adversaries, and among these many harboured well-founded doubts on the Ptolemaic or Tychonic systems. In effect, it was not at all clear "what" was to be condemned and why it should be condemned. A scientific opinion? Can a scientific opinion be an object of faith? The question from the theological and religious point of view was complex: there were currents of thought based on an authoritative Catholic tradition that were in favour of Galileo, and these were being examined and studied in depth. The discussion could not be restricted to the Roman theologians, who headed the Congregation of the Inquisition and the Index. The condemnation, therefore, did not have a "theological and religious maturation" and from this point of view, it did not reveal the opinion of the Church, simply because such an opinion had not yet been formulated and had had no time to find expression. In effect the error was not so much that of the theologians but of those who took on the responsibility for the decision without waiting for the Church as an ecclesiastical community, to express its certain mind.

2. The Copernican theories and the Church

In order to understand the premises of the Galileo issue, we must give some attention to certain matters relating to the spread of the Copernican thesis and the publication of his work, *De revolutionibus orbium coelestium.* As is well known, Copernicus began to make public his thesis concerning the new heliocentric concept of the universe in a brief explanation called the *Commentariolus,* which circulated exclusively in manuscript copy between 1512 and 1515. But his fame as an expert astronomer had already reached Rome, so that Bishop Paul of Middelburg, the president of the Commission of the fifth Lateran Council (1514) which had been charged with the reform of the calendar, had invited him to take part in its work, and to communicate his opinions on the matter.[8] As Copernicus himself recalls, he did not send a proposal because he believed that it was not possible to proceed to reform without first knowing with greater exactitude the movements of the moon and sun. In this way he showed that reserve which surrounded all his work and ideas, which were only published on the insistence of his friends, under the protection of the Church Authorities and thanks to the assistance of his faithful pupil, Rheticus. The interest in ecclesiastical circles in the Curia in Copernicus' astronomic researches, despite the fact that he did not take part in the work of the commission, always remained intense. In 1533, Albert Widmanstadt, secretary of Clement VII, illustrated the Copernican system to the Pope in the presence of Cardinal Salviati and other curial dignitaries in the gardens of the Vatican. He explained the system as it had appeared in the *Commentariolus*,[9] and three years later, on 1st November 1536, Cardinal Nicholas Schönberg, most probably on the instance of Paul III himself, wrote to Copernicus, exhorting him to communicate the results of his work to all learned persons, and so to publish them. In the meantime he wished to have, at his own expense, a manuscript copy of the work in question: "I have come to hear that not only do you know in depth the teachings of the ancient mathematicians, but that you have created a new theory of the universe according to which the Earth moves and the Sun occupies the fundamental and thus central position [...] moreover that you have written a treatise on this entirely new astronomical theory, and also calculated the movements of the planets, the tables of which you have established to the great admiration of all. For this reason, learned sir, without wishing to be importunate, I would ask you insistently to communicate your discovery to the scientific world, and to send me as soon as possible your theories on the universe, together with the tables and everything that you have on this subject".[10]

Meanwhile Copernicus, who was requested to do this in a friendly manner, but nevertheless felt under pressure, by his superior Bishop Giese, and by Rheticus, had decided to put in print a first "representation" of his astronomic system, under the form of a letter addressed by Rheticus to his professor of astronomy and mathematics, Johannes Schœner. This came out in February 1540 and contributed to reviving interest in the new astronomic concepts, and consequently led to new pressure on Copernicus to decide finally to print the long-awaited work. But among all this support, not least that coming from the Holy See itself, there were also, already, the first criticisms, and specifically on the point which was then to constitute the main motif of the Galileo question, i.e. the relationship between the heliocentric idea and Scripture. Even Luther had intervened; in 1539 he had given a somewhat crude judgment on the new astronomic theory: "There is talk of a new astronomer, who seeks to show that the earth moves instead of the sun, and the moon […] This imbecile wants to turn the whole art of astronomy head over heels. Only that, and the Holy Scriptures tell us so, it is the Sun that Joshua ordered to stand still, and not the Earth". Other observations on the part of Melancthon had followed this.[11] The Fathers of the reformation had taken up a position quite contrary to the Copernican notion, but this did not stop the protestant Rheticus, who was backed by Melancthon, becoming the publisher of *De revolutionibus*. In fact in the end Copernicus had decided on the publication of his work, but because he knew that he would meet up with the opposition of the Aristotelians sooner or later, as well as that of the theologians – initially the protestants, but then perhaps those from the Catholic side too – he had asked permission (and been allowed) to dedicate his work to the Pope, Paul III Farnese. In the dedication he did not omit to underline the conflict which existed between his conceptions and established doctrine on, the theological and religious plane, and he confided in the benevolence and protection of the Pontiff, who would keep him safe from future attacks by those who, in ignorance of mathematics, nevertheless spoke of things about which they knew nothing: "[…] possibly there may be babblers who, although completely ignorant of mathematics, yet claim to stand in judgment, because of some passage of scripture poorly interpreted in their favour and thus dare to reassume and prescribe these conclusions of mine". Copernicus recalled how his work had found practical inspiration in the widely felt need for the reform of the calendar. In fact he believed he had made an important contribution to the solution of the complex problems relating to the determining of the length of the years and months and the movements of the sun and moon, indispensable preconditions for the new calendar.[12]

In fact, Copernicus had for some time been concerned with the negative reception of his new conception of the universe, with the criticisms of his thesis, and in the years which preceded the publication of *De revolutionibus*, he spoke of this with this most trusted friends and with one of the representative and authoritative protestants, Nicola Osiander. Thus, in the *Esposizione dei libri sulle Rivoluzioni,* edited by Rheticus, we immediately find the intention to "attenuate" the novelty of Copernicus' conception, and to present it almost as a perfection and continuation of the astronomy of Ptolemy, in line with the Platonic notion of a geometrically structured universe, already in some ways previously announced by astronomers of the Pythagorean school. Moreover, Rheticus had composed an essay dedicated specifically at demonstrating the compatibility of the notions of his master with those passages of the Bible which seemed to affirm that stable state of the earth. He refers to the discussions which had taken place between himself, Copernicus and Bishop Giese, and how, solely thanks to the authoritative insistence and reasoning of the latter, the scientist had decided to publish his work.[13] Basically, the meaning of these testimonies, as also of the publication of the letter of Cardinal Schönberg and the the dedication to the Pope, was that the merit of and responsibility for the publication of *De revolutionibus* should be attributed to the church authorities.

With Osiander, Copernicus had initiated a correspondence some years before the printing of his works, in order to have the opinion of the theologian about the criticism which the *De revolutionibus* might meet with; evidently he sought an authoritative guarantor among the Protestants as well. Osiander advised both Copernicus and Rheticus to emphasise the strictly hypothetical nature of the theses which referred to the new helio-centric system: these, therefore, served only to provide an "explanation" of astronomic phenomena, valid solely for the purpose of a more exact calculation of the movements of the planets and the sun, but without any pretence of stating its true correspondence to the natural state of things. With these specific points made, Osiander took on the responsibility of having printed, in a celebrated Protestant press at Nuremburg, the *De revolutionibus* and for greater caution he thought it would be wise to follow the advice which he had showed to the scientist and his pupil, by introducing a preface to the book, edited by himself and not signed, in which the considerations that he had referred to by letter had taken form.[14]

In substance, the preface reasserted the classical distinction between physics or natural philosophy, the object of which is true knowledge – i.e. what corresponds to the reality of nature, and astronomy as a discipline aimed at calculating, through mathematics and geometry, the movement of the stars, as they appear to our vision. The notions that we form to explain these movements only serve to "save the phenomena", to give them a rational interpretation, valid for the geometric representation of movement, and for the subsequent mathematical calculation. These cannot, however, give us any useful indications about the "real nature" of astronomic phenomena. It is on the basis of these points that the new astronomic theory of Copernicus must be understood; it does not, therefore, refer to the true nature of the planetary system.

Osiander's preface, very probably published without Copernicus' knowledge (he was dying while the printing of his work was being completed), aroused very lively protests, as is well known, from those who held that the scientist had, on the contrary, maintained that the helio-centric notion did in fact correspond to the reality of the planetary system. Copernicus had undoubtedly intended by his work to overcome the traditional notion of a clear separation between physics and astronomy, the first being a science of nature and the second the science of calculating the movements of the planets. He wished to substitute an astronomic physics, based on the mathematico-geometrical structure of the universe, even though the study of the movement of the planets conducted in the fifth and sixth books could give the impression that the geometrical description of movements based on the epicycles of Ptolemy had a merely hypothetical value.[15] The first to protest, in fact, was Bishop Giese himself, who wrote to Rheticus with the aim of having the false doctrine denounced to the Senate of Nuremburg. The attempt by Bishop Giese to force the printer to correct the edition had no outcome; thus the preface by Osiander was not removed; very probably it was seen as a "password" for a work which had aroused the criticism of leading exponents of the Reformation, a necessary warning which would, after all, favour the spread of scientific knowledge which would be useful to all the nations.[16]

De revolutionibus did not match up to the expectations, or to the enthusiasm of Copernicus' friends: it had a limited circulation, solely among the "members of the trade". The new revolutionary theory of the planetary system left the learned world to a great extent indifferent, and to judge from the number of editions of the traditional texts, based so to speak on the Ptolemaic system, the scientific establishment of the time paid little attention to the Copernican theses, and seemed to take on board the considerations of Osiander. The fame of Copernicus became widespread and consolidated above all because of the contribution which the work had made to the calculation of the orbits and the astronomic tables, which published by Reinhold, a colleague of

Rheticus, in Wittenberg, were welcomed with great favour by astronomers, so as to be nick-named the *calculatio copernicana.* These would have been the bases for the reform of the calendar. It may be added that the very accurate astronomical researches of Tycho Brache, while they were the premises for the work of Kepler, and hence the presupposition for the discovery of the three laws on which the planetary system is founded as it was proposed by Copernicus, also served to uphold the notion that the problems posed by Copernicus could have been resolved by a system in which the planets orbited around the sun, and the latter, with all the planets, around the earth, which would hence remain at the centre of the universe.[17] The idea of Tycho thus contributed to fostering the notion that astronomic ideas were hypotheses, "fictions" useful only for the calculation of the movement of the planets, while it brought to light thanks to the greater precision and continuity of the astronomic measurements, inconsistencies and contradictions in the Copernican system.

3. Galileo and the heliocentric hypothesis: agreements and criticisms

At the end of the sixteenth century, only a few astronomers accepted the Copernican system, while the majority rejected it, while nevertheless recognising Copernicus' very great merits as a "calculator". As far as Italy is concerned, we have only to remember the judgments of Clavius and Magini, among the best known astronomers and mathematicians, who while they stressed the importance of the contribution made by *De revolutionibus,* did not consider that they could accept the heliocentric hypothesis which in their opinion had been developed by extremely complex geometric proofs sometimes in contradiction of one another.[18]

Galileo's first testimony in favour of the Copernican thesis is to be found in a letter to Jacopo Mazzoni dated 30th May 1597. His friend had illustrated a natural phenomenon recorded by ancient writers (the peak of the Caucasus is illuminated by the sun's rays while on the plain below evening has already fallen) in order to criticise the Copernican system, and Galileo replied to the sending of this note by proposing a different interpretation which, in fact, supported the heliocentric thesis: "[...] which (is) held by me to be more probable than the other of Aristotle and Ptolemy".[19] After several months he returned to the question of Copernicus: in August 1597, replying to Keppler to thank him for sending the *Mysterium Cosmographicum*, he restated his "Copernicanism" and told his illustrious correspondent that he had made on his own account a series of considerations in defence of the heliocentric system, but did not believe that he could publish them because of the suspicion and absolute incomprehension with which they would have been greeted by "an infinite multitude (for such is the number of fools for whom Copernicus was an object of ridicule and derision)".[20] Nothing remained, therefore, but to leave the defence of Copernicus in the drawer since unfortunately, there were not many like Keppler willing to defend Copernicus' ideas.

A reply which undoubtedly raised some concern, also because Galileo did not answer the second letter from his illustrious colleague, the imperial mathematician. In this letter Keppler exhorted him to join him in carrying on together the "battle" in favour of Copernicus, and concluded: "Let me know, at least in private if you do not want to do so in public, what you have discovered in support of Copernicus".[21] Galileo did not think it was appropriate to follow up his correspondence with Keppler on such a contentious and compromising issue for a young professor who, teaching in Padua, found himself in the situation of Daniel in the lions' den, surrounded on all sides by the most qualified and infuriated representatives of ultra-orthodox Artistotelianism.

Unfortunately his considerations on the defence of Copernicus have not come down to us among his writings from the Padua period, but only a course of lectures held in 1604, *Trattato sulla sfera,* in which he expounds the Ptolemaic system without any reference to that of Copernicus and Tycho Brahe. The initial nucleus of Galileo's scientific interest, as is well known, concerned mathematics and physics, with special reference to movement and its problems, and the subsequent critique of the dominant Aristotelian method, which stood in the way of the acquisition of experimental data: "he was not a 'born astronomer', like Copernicus, Rheticus, Tycho Brahe and Kepler.[22] Very probably his first interest in Copernicus arose from the fact that the heliocentric thesis was radically opposed to the Aristotelian conception of the universe; his initial Copernicanism was actually anti-Aristotelian in essence. He cannot have paid much attention to the complex geometric proofs of the movement of the planets, which had as its premises the calculations relating to the orbits, in contrast to Kepler, who was seeking for the laws of planetary motion in order to explain by mathematical formulae and geometric relations, the data which had been obtained on the basis of calculations.

Galileo, on the other hand, was inclined towards a science in which mathematics and geometry were intimately connected with experimental datum, and it was probably this which, according to his scientific inclinations, was missing from theories of *De revolutionibus* and the *Mysterium Cosmographicum.* Very probably for this reason, he did not follow up the invitation by Kepler to collaborate in the defence and diffusion of the Copernican system. Only after the invention of the telescope and the discoveries which derived from astronomical observations did Galileo succeed in obtaining the experimental data which allowed him to demonstrate, according to his own scientific convictions, the truth of the heliocentric thesis, and to be able to take up a public position in favour of the Copernican system. The *Nuncius sidereus* made a profound impression on public opinion, it aroused a very lively interest in all those who were interested in a more or less professional way in astronomy and scientific issues. It had a "breakthrough" effect far superior to that of *De revolutionibus* or to that of Kepler's *Mysterium Cosmographicum;* in fact it was based on data which could be obtained by all, which were not founded on complex and subtle mathematico-geometric proofs, but on direct observation, and which demonstrated with immediate effect the inconsistency of the Aristotelian concept of the universe. The echo of the discoveries even reached Campanella, then a prisoner in the Castel dell'Uovo, who wrote a letter to Galileo in which he bore witness to his enthusiasm for the great discoveries and suggested to him – for the time being – scriptural arguments in defence of the new astronomical theories.[23]

Only after the *Nuncius sidereus,* after acquiring elements of proof based on direct observation, did Galileo publicly uphold the truth of the Copernican thesis. He wrote of it to Clavius in December 1610: "Now you can see clearly how Venus (and there can be no doubt that the same applies to Mercury) goes around the sun, the centre beyond all doubt of the maximum revolutions of all the planets […] and how this system of planets is surely of a different manner from what is commonly supposed […]".[24] And a short time afterwards, he expressed an identical judgment in a letter addressed in January 1611 to Giuliano de' Medici, ambassador in Prague, even though he made no secret of the criticisms of the "philosophers *in libris*", whom he now felt strong enough to face and counter with arguments based on the data discovered through his telescopic observations: "[…] the other, that Venus most necessarily revolves around the sun, like Mercury and all the other planets, something rightly believed by Pythagoras, Copernicus, Kepler and myself, but not yet judiciously proven. So Herr Kepler and the other Copernicans have reason for congratulation in having believed, and philosophised well, even though it has fallen to us, and will fall to us again, to be reputed by the generality of philosophers *in libris* as men of little understanding and little more than fools".[25] And again, to Paolo Sarpi in February 1611: "while we consider that in fact it is very true that all the planets revolve around the sun as the centre of their orbits […], now here we see for certain that Venus does revolve around the sun […]";[26] statements which he repeated in two letters to Marco Welser on the discovery of sunspots, in an argument with Scheiner.[27]

The discoveries of Galileo had full recognition in academic and ecclesiastical circles in Rome. From April to May 1611, the scientist from Pisa was in Rome, welcomed with the most lively interest and with great acclaim. He was inscribed in the Accademia dei Lincei, recently constituted on the initiative of the Cesi princes, and was received on 22nd April by Paul V himself, who as a sign of particular consideration "did not permit me to say even a single word while kneeling";[28] he had a chance to meet Cardinals Del Monte, Maffeo Barberini, Borghese, Conti, Montalto, Farnese, Aquaviva, Orsini, Jouyeuse and Bandini, to whom he reported and demonstrated his discoveries. Finally in a meeting of academics held in the Collegio Romano, the *Nuncius sidereus* and his theory on the floating of bodies were presented and discussed.[29] Although Galileo had already shown his Copernican leanings, to which he almost certainly referred during his stay in Rome, there were no observations or reservations of a theological kind about Galileo's discoveries on the part of the Church, and especially on the part of the Jesuit astronomers and scientists.

The first criticisms famously came from the secular world; from an Aristotelian "of strict obedience". In 1610-1611 a dissertation in manuscript form, *Contro il moto della terra,* by Ludovico delle Colombe was in circulation.[30] Without naming Galileo, it not only reasserted the traditional arguments in favour of the "stability" of the earth, but it supplemented them with an appeal to passages of Scripture from which such notions could be deduced. This essay did not trouble Galileo: he referred it to his friend Gallanzoni in July 1611, asking him to show it to Cardinal Francesco de Joyeuse, pointing out the complete ignorance on the part of Ludovico delle Colombe of the Copernican system, and concluding that the dissertation did not merit any reply.[31]

But there was no lack of those among Galileo's friends who believed, on the contrary, that it was necessary to be prudent, and to treat the question with great discretion, because in effect it was very delicate. "That the earth turns" wrote Paolo Gualdo from Padua in May 1611, "up to now, I have found no philosopher nor astrologer of any kind to subscribe to your opinion, and even less will the theologians wish to do so: think carefully, then, before assertively stating this opinion of yours in public as the truth, because many things can be said by way of dispute, so that it is not wise to assert it as truth, especially when the universal opinion of all is against it, soaked up, so to speak, *ab orbe condito".*[32] The fears of his friend from Padua were soon to find a confirmation: from Rome, in December of the same year, Ludovico Cigoli warned Galileo that in Florence "a certain line-up of the malign and those envious of your virtue and merits have gathered together, and at their head is the Archbishop, and they are roaming about in a rage trying to find something to latch on to about the movement of the earth and other things [...]".[33] The opening of hostilities was at hand, then, with the effort to bring the discussion back, or rather to reduce it, to the theological and religious issue.

The echoes of the discussions held in academic and theological circles in Florence must have reached Rome, for a friend of the scientist, Monsignor Giovan Battista Agucchi,[34] who had followed the astronomic discoveries with great interest and carried on some astronomic observations himself with great diligence as a learned amateur, contacted Galileo in July 1613 to communicate to him his impressions of the debate going on concerning the Copernican system. It is a letter that allows us a glimpse into the attitude of interest, of open-ness, almost, to the Galileo thesis which inspired well-qualified members of the ecclesiastical circle. They recognised the importance of Galileo's astronomical discoveries, but nevertheless had the impression that the Copernican thesis was not yet backed by sure and conclusive proofs.

The discussions, disputes, and the struggles did not trouble the Monsignor. Indeed there is no truth which has not been disputed: his impression is that in the state of awareness, or at least his state of awareness, the question seemed incapable of resolution on the plane of authority – i.e. on the basis of a judgment by a scientist whose work would be validated by the consensus of the majority. He admits that he has never given much credence to the Copernican theories, but after hearing that Galileo approves and upholds them, he has begun to consider them with some attention. But he is not yet able to feel fully convinced: "Your authority alone, since I have discovered that you held similar opinions, moves me to bend my spirit to them, but not in such a way that I have not, even so, some doubts, and do not lean rather to the other side, to which three principal reasons urge me. The first is the authority of Holy Scripture, which in several places, and with great clarity, states the contrary [...] The second reason is the authority of all the most esteemed mathematicians who have lived from the time of Copernicus to the present. [...]".

In this situation, Agucchi holds that reference must first of all be had to demonstrations "with mathematical proofs, and by way of sense and well-based experience which convinces", but when these demonstrations are not provided, then authority sub-enters. Faced with the particular opinions of individuals, "no other way remains to us in the end to determine, not necessarily demonstrated by science, than the sole authority considered best by the majority and the most esteemed, because we wish to believe that the truth, however ambiguous, is revealed by universal and harmonious opinion. Now among all those astronomers, I hold Tycho in great esteem, for he has triumphed in the past by diligence in observing the heavenly motions". The perplexity felt by Agucchi thus arises from the fact that the scrupulous astronomic observations of Tycho Brahe had not succeeded in confirming the Copernican system. He thus expressed the need to wait, and at the same time formulated a hope that Galileo was in a position to provide the necessary mathematical proofs – conforming, moreover to his scientific principles – to demonstrate the Copernican theory. He did not hide his doubts about the fact that the traditional opinion in favour of a geocentric system could be abandoned only on the basis of probable arguments: "[...] because if it does not prove to be the case that it can be demonstrated by mathematical and necessary proofs, it would be impossible for the world to be persuaded by only probable reasons; such a thing would not very easily enter into the human intellect".[35] Agucchi thus saw very clearly the terms in which from then onwards for quite a few years, the Copernican question would be placed before the ecclesiastical authorities.

4. Denunciation to the Holy Office

In the environment that prevailed in Florence and Pisa in 1612-13, there was constant discussion of the daring ideas of the Grand Duke's own mathematician and philosopher; so much so that the Rector of the University of Pisa, Arturo d'Elci – who was also a rigid Artistotelian – decided to warn Castelli as he was about to begin teaching, "not to enter into opinions about the motions of the earth".[36] In the end, these reservations and criticisms were voiced only within the ambit of the Grand Duke's family.

In the first days of December 1613, Castelli had taken part in a luncheon at the Grand Duke's palace, and on that occasion, either the Grand Duke himself or his mother, Christine of Lorraine, had asked for information about the satellites of Jupiter. On this matter, they questioned another of the diners, a lecturer at the University of Pisa, Cosimo Boscaglia, who confirmed Galileo's discoveries, but could not resist whispering "something in the ear of Madame, and acknowledging the truth of the heavenly novelties that had been discovered by Your Excellency, saying that only the movement of the earth still seemed to be unbelievable, and indeed could not be believed, since the Holy Scriptures were manifestly contrary to such a view". The conversation did not end there, and there was a follow-up: when the meal was over, Castelli did not have time to leave the palace before he was summoned and then accompanied to the Grand Duke's own chamber, where, in the presence of Duke Cosimo himself, his wife, Madame Christine, Antonio de' Medici, Paolo Giordano Orsini and Boscaglia, he had to follow for two hours while the problem of the relations between the heliocentric system and the Scriptures was demonstrated: [...] the grand Duke and the Archduchess were of my part" Castelli reported to Galileo, "and Signor Paolo Giordano came to my defence with a passage of Scripture which was directly relevant. Only Madama Serenissima remained to contradict me, but in such a way that I was able to get her to listen to me. Sirgnor Boscaglia refrained from any contradiction".[37]

Galileo immediately replied with a long letter to Castelli, in which he dealt with the question of the relations between the Copernican system and Scripture:[38] the episode had struck him and worried him very deeply, above all because of the attitude of the Grand Duke's mother. He was well ware that it was not only his own prestige that was on the line, but also his future as a scientist, which was by now closely linked to the faith and esteem – and hence the favour and protection – of the House of Medici. He knew that the young Grand Duke's family could not and would not run the risk of a serious political and religious dispute with Rome, as sponsors of opinions that were evidently bold, and possibly heretical. The interest that he had demonstrated in the theological and religious aspects of the heliocentric theory was proof of this.

Galileo was thus "constrained" to intervene in the discussion – initiated moreover by his adversaries with the aim of combating him on the religious plane – to demonstrate the full legitimacy of his conceptions in the light of a correct exegesis of Scripture. Initially it was a matter of reassuring the Grand Duke, the Archduchess and Madame Christine of his sincere adhesion to the principles of Catholicism, and of the fact that no contradiction existed between Scripture and his astronomic notions, above all because the former refers to what pertains to our faith, and certainly does not concern questions of a scientific nature.

As Cardinal Baronio had said: "the intention of Holy Scripture is to instruct us how to go to heaven, not how the heavens go".[39] So Galileo had to justify himself before the Medici from the theological and religious standpoints, and at the same time he had to provide them with a valid rationale in the face of the ecclesiastical authorities, above all those of Rome. He had to justify the favour which was being shown to his studies and scientific researches. This, it seems to me, is the real motive which induced Galileo to approach the Copernican question from a theological and religious point of view, in order to stress the distinction which it was necessary to maintain between theology, philosophy and science, and thus to sketch out a solution which would define, with clarity, the fields proper to each of these disciplines. It was necessary to ensure that scientific questions were not reduced to problems of Scriptural exegesis.

Galileo cannot therefore be reproached with lack of prudence; he was not guilty of pride and a punctilious claim to have his reasoning recognised at all times and in all places, even when it had shaky foundations. He cannot be blamed for having initiated a polemic on the level of the radical contradiction – truth on the one side, error on the other – without having genuinely conclusive proofs in favour of his thesis, which would have provoked the intervention and condemnation of the ecclesiastical authority. The insinuations and criticisms of his adversaries had brought him face to face, as a Catholic and a scientist, with the problem of the relations between science and Scripture, and thus between science and faith. He had to find a solution which would satisfy his own conscience, and propose it above all to those who at that moment represented the State and assumed the responsibility for fostering his scientific programme. Nor could he fail to uphold it before the ecclesiastical authorities: for the sake of consistency in his own convictions, he could not admit that an opinion which he held to be in error should be put forward as the truth.

The debate and the consequent polemic did not arise, as the Tuscan ambassador in Rome, Paolo Guicciardini, held, from the "passionate and finicky" character of Galileo "[…] and Monsignor Cardinal dal (*sic*) Monte and I, to the small extent we could, and several cardinals of the Sacred Office, have tried to persuade him to calm down, and not pick away at this matter, but if he wished to hold this opinion, then to hold it privately, without making such an effort to dispose and draw others to hold the same […]. But he has become inflamed in his opinions, he has great passion within him, and little strength and prudence to enable him to win […]".[40] The discussion arose out of the interest which Galileo's discoveries had aroused in the world of astronomy, which had become almost the "great fact" of the day, from the problems it had raised and the reactions which it had aroused, which had finally involved the Holy Office, thanks initially to the denunciation of Fr Lorini, and then to the more sober-minded one of Fr Caccini. The Holy Office would probably have preferred to do without dealing with such a matter.

Certainly Galileo, mindful of the great successes he had achieved in 1611, held that this was a good occasion to win again, to triumph finally over his adversaries, and finally to get the Copernican system recognised by the ecclesiastical authorities. He moved, basically, as a Counter-Reformation Catholic, with the zeal and spirit of proselytism, because this was a matter of combating error, of preventing it from being assumed as truth, which would thus diminish the prestige of the Church authorities and eventually of Scripture itself. This was the reason he could not remain silent; and could not accept the logic of the State policy which his ambassador was suggesting to him, not because he was "stubbornly determined to convince the friars". Galileo also had a taste for Academe: he liked to give life to a debate, and enjoyed the tension of a duel of oratory, in which he knew he was a great expert and could beat his adversaries when they least expected it: (i.e. when they held that they had confuted him), by showing in a few phrases the inconsistencies of their notions: he had his secret weapons, with which he knew how to 'wound' those who contradicted him, provoking jealousy, rancour and resentment. And all this would naturally have its weight in the way things worked out.

Between December 1615 and February 1616, while the Congregation of the Holy Office was seeking to find a solution to this thorny question, Galileo was the "matador" of the Copernican system: he "represented" it in the academies, in the salons of Rome, always receiving admiration from his listeners for his art in discourse, and an ill-concealed aversion among his incautious opponents. One witness of these debates, Canon Antonio Querengo, tells us: "We have here Galileo, who often, in gatherings of men of curious intellect, makes amazing speeches about the opinion of Copernicus, believed by him to be the truth […].[41] Your Most Illustrious Excellency (Cardinal Alessandro d'Este) would greatly enjoy it if you were to hear him discourse, as he does, in the midst of fifteen or twenty who make cruel assaults on him, sometimes in one house and sometimes in another. But he is fortified in such a way that he laughs at them all; and even though the novelty of his opinion may not persuade, he does make the best part of the arguments which his opponents try to hurl against him seem like vanity. On Monday, in particular, in the house of Sig. Federico Ghislieri, he offered wonderful proofs; and what pleased me very much was that before replying to the opposing arguments, he blew them up and reinforced them with new bases of apparently huge proportions, only then to overturn them and make his adversaries seem even more ridiculous".[42]

The animated and fascinating discussions of the academies and the Roman salons certainly did not resolve the question, which had by now been formally raised by the Dominicans of Santa Maria Novella. In the early days of February 1615, Fr Lorini had written to Cardinal Paolo Sfondrati, Prefect of the Congregation for the Index, to point out to him the spread of Galileo's letter to Castelli, in which there was a defence of the Copernican system, and an interpretation of Scripture contrary to the consolidated teaching of tradition. He specified, however, that he did not intend to make a formal denunciation, but only to call the attention of the church authorities, for an eventual and more thorough examination on the part of the Congregation for the Index.[43] Since this was a matter pertaining to the faith, and the letter was not printed, Sfondrati thought it was wise to interest Cardinal Millini in the matter. Millini was Secretary of the Congregation of the Holy Office, and he opened the way for Lorini's denunciation. Once a reliable copy of Galileo's letter to Castelli had been acquired, one of the Consultants of the Congregation was charged with preparing a preliminary opinion. Without entering specifically into the Copenican question, he said that he did not see in Galileo's notions any statement which was worthy of censure: Galileo "though sometimes he makes improper use of words, does not however deviate (*a semitis*) from Catholic language".[44] It seemed then that the question should be concluded in the investigatory stage, if it had not been for the fact that in those very days Fr Caccini happened to come to Rome, and after consulting with Cardinal Galamini, requested and obtained a hearing from the General Commissariat of the Holy Office. On 20th March, in a detailed deposition, he referred to the discussions which had arisen in Florence concerning

Galileo's theses, which "according to my conscience and intelligence, are repugnant to Sacred Scripture as expounded by the Holy Fathers".[45] This was the way in which the first trial of Galileo was brought about; it was to conclude in March 1616, and during it the problem of the relation between the Copernican thesis and the traditional interpretation of certain passages of Scripture was discussed and examined in depth. Such a discussion was lacking in the second trial of 1633, which was to have an exclusively disciplinary character.

5. The Letter to Madame Christine: *the conception of the universe and the Scriptures. St Augustine, St Thomas*

Galileo's line of defence, mentioned in the letter to Castelli, had been taken up again and systematically expounded, as is well known, in the *Letter to Madame Christine,* in which the problem of the relations between theology, biblical exegesis, philosophy and natural science had been basically interpreted and resolved in the light of a line of thought first set out by Augustine in his commentary on Genesis. This had been accepted by the subsequent patristic tradition, and resumed authoritatively by St Thomas. Perhaps it was this which was the motive that the first consideration by the Holy Office did not find any notions to censure in the letter to Castelli, which contains the essential points of Galileo's arguments as set out in the *Letter to Madame Christine.*

As is well known, the problem of the relationship between science and Scripture was dealt with by St Augustine in his commentary on the Book of Genesis. The cosmological conception of the Bible – the flat earth surmounted by the vault of the heavens – contrasted radically with the Greek view – in which the earth and the planets were spherical in form and endowed with circular motion – and it was therefore a matter of setting down the criteria to be followed in interpreting Scripture, when the text referred to natural phenomena, and especially astronomical ones.[46] St Augustine begins from the consideration that between the truth, which is known and perceived through human reason, and the revelation, no conflict exists. So that when a truth of nature is discovered or demonstrated, the truths of faith as founded on the Word are not involved or contradicted in any way. It is necessary, therefore, always to keep in mind the distinction between what refers to the faith and what refers to the knowledge of nature.[47]

St Augustine held that when, in commenting on Scripture, one met with statements which concerned natural phenomena of which we cannot have direct experience, such as those of astronomy, which thus pose "difficult and obscure questions, very far removed from us", we must adopt an approach of great prudence and caution; much better not to involve ourselves in any opinions, and above all not involve the authority of Scripture and run the risk of substituting our own private opinions for the authority of Scripture. On the other hand as has been mentioned, the truth about facts of nature when they are discovered does not contradict in any way the truths of faith affirmed by the Scriptures, while error, when it is recognised as such, ends up by rendering the person who has maintained it as if it were truth odious.[48] In the *De Actis contra Felicem Manichaeum,* Augustine stresses very clearly the principle that Scripture must not be considered as a text from which scientific knowledge about nature can be derived: *"Non legitur in Evangelio Dominum dixisse: Mitto vobis Paracletum qui vos doceat de cursu solis et lunae; christianos enim facere volebat non mathematicos. Sufficit autem ut homines de his rebus quantum in schola didicerunt noverint propter humanos usus".*[49]

The Augustinian notion that a substantial distinction must be maintained between the truths of faith and those of human reason, to avoid doubt and misunderstandings which would end up by undermining the authority of Scripture, is taken up again by St Thomas in the debate which was aroused by a direct knowledge of the Aristotelian concept of cosmology as opposed to that of Ptolemy. It is well known that the former formulated a physical explanation of the universe and of the movement of the stars, while the latter calculated the motion of the stars on the basis of astronomic phenomena, and gave a simply mathematical-geometric explanation of it. According to one of the commentators of Aristotle, Simplicius, this has a merely hypothetical value; it is an abstraction, a mathematical fiction which has no correspondence with reality. In fact, Ptolemy had introduced into the movement of the planets around the earth, a complex system of cycles and epicycles which could not be reconciled with the Aristotelian notion of a homocentric cosmos.[50]

St Thomas, taking up the considerations made by Simplicius, held that the Ptolemaic system is founded on hypotheses (*suppositiones*) which have no relation with natural reality, but which serve only to save the phenomena: i.e. to give them a geometrical explanation, aimed at calculating the movement of the planets. It must also be admitted though that the astronomic teachings of Aristotle are also substantially founded on hypotheses, which, however, the great philosopher believed corresponded to reality and were therefore true. The movements of the planets, on the other hand, can be explained in a more convincing way than that of either Aristotle or Ptolemy, which astronomers have not yet been able to discover.[51]

Scientific research concerning the planetary system for St Thomas remained open: the Aristotelian/Ptolemaic notion of the universe had a hypothetical value, and as such needed to be perfected by scientific research. Founded on human reason, the latter has a sphere of autonomy, which has to do with the distinction between theology and philosophy, between reason and faith. Thus, we cannot resolve the questions which refer to natural truths on the basis of the principles of faith, and consequently we must proceed with great caution when it is a matter of judging on the basis of Scripture questions which have to do with natural phenomena. Referring explicitly to St Augustine, St Thomas puts the interpreter of Scripture on guard against the negative consequences that derive from maintaining or rejecting, as if they belonged to Christian doctrine, statements which do not concern religion. Philosophical teachings cannot be maintained or rejected because they share in or deny the truths of faith. We could commit grievous errors by upholding hypotheses which have no rational foundation or denying truths which have been solidly established by human reason. Both in the first and second cases, we end up by rendering the Christian doctrine less credible, by offering reasons which can be used against it.[52] A very appropriate warning, which arose out of the need felt by Thomas to guarantee the rights of reason from the temptation to give absolute value to the evidence of Christian faith and spirituality in opposition to the reality of the human world.

6. The Copernican question and the Scriptures: M. Cano, D. da Zuñica, P. Pázmány, P. A. Foscarini, T. Campanella

The exegetical criteria which were put forward by the thinking of St Augustine and St Thomas found a natural complement in the critical and philosophical requirements that belong to humanism, which demands recourse to all the assistance that can be given by philosophy, science, and history, permitting a better understanding of the biblical text. This, in fact, is the thesis upheld by Melchior Cano, the authoritative Spanish theologian of the sixteenth century. He stressed how important it was from the point of view of correct biblical exegesis, that the work of the interpreter should have a sure rational and scientific foundation. Among other things he advised that even the interpretations of the Fathers should be accepted with prudence, because they had only limited preparation in philosophy and natural science. The Bible cannot be interpreted by limiting oneself to the data which emerge from the literal text and by referring then to the comments of the Fathers; there are in fact many questions which can only be resolved with the assistance of philosophy, mathematics, geometry and astronomy. At times there are references in Scripture to natural phenomena in terms of miracles which can only be understood correctly on the basis of philosophy and natural science. These are necessary to the theologian; if man is a rational being, Cano concludes, the theologian cannot judge on the basis of authority alone.[53]

The exegetical tendency advocated by Melchior was also followed by another Spanish theologian, the Dominican Diego da Zuñica, with reference specifically to the questions arising from the Copernican thesis.[54] In his *Commentary on the Book of Job,* published in Toledo in 1584, the Spanish theologian considers Chapter 9, verse 6: "Who moved the earth from its place", and says that this statement could only be explained if the Copernican heliocentric notion, with the movement of the earth, was accepted: this passage, in fact, in contrast with others in which the immobility of the earth is asserted, refers explicitly to its movement. Zuñica does not hesitate to declare his full adherence to the Copernican thesis, which, moreover, takes up once more what had already been maintained by the Pythagoreans, and which allows us a more convincing explanation of numerous astronomical phenomena, especially that of determining accurately the beginning of the solar year, with a clear reference to the reform of the calendar which had recently been carried out. It also refers to the calculations taken from *De revolutionibus* for the preparatory work of this important undertaking.[55]

As far as the other passages of Scripture are concerned, in which movements of the sun and the immobility of the earth are mentioned, it must be observed that the expression of *Ecclesiastes*, "But the earth standeth eternally", must be interpreted in a figurative sense, with reference to the generations of mankind which pass away, while only the earth remains – "standeth eternally". The other passages use a current way of speaking of which Copernicus himself also makes use, by which we attribute the movements of the earth to the sun. It should be noted that the comments of Zuñica, approved by the Spanish church authorities (by the Jesuit College of Madrid, by the Archbishop of Toledo, Cardinal Gaspare de Quiroga, and by the Provincial of the Augustinians in Aragon) must have enjoyed a certain measure of success in ecclesiastical circles, since it was published in a new edition in Rome in 1591, with the approval of the Roman censors, and under the high patronage of Gregory XV himself. Between 1584 and 1591, the ecclesiastical authorities in Toledo, Madrid and Rome had in substance accepted the principle that passages of Scripture which referred to the movements of the sun could be interpreted in the light of the conclusions of the Copernican theory.

This trend in exegesis found further confirmation in the commentary on Artistotle's *De coelo,* which was composed on the occasion of the university courses held at Graz between 1597 and 1607 by the Hungarian Jesuit, Pietro Pázmány.[56] In the years that followed, he was to have an essential role in the reorganisation of Catholicism in his country. Pázmány maintained that the differing theories which existed to explain the cosmological notions of Aristotle must be considered in the light of mere mathematical hypotheses, and in this context he referred to the *Theoriche* of Alessandro Piccolomini, who had in fact called his students' attention to the fact that the cycles and epicycles of Ptolemy, like other astronomers, did not pose any problems concerning their correspondence with natural reality, concerning falsehood or truth, but served only to "save the phenomena", to give them an interpretation for the purposes of astronomical calculation.[57] Among the various hypotheses formulated to explain the movements of the planets, Pázmány laid particular stress on the Copernican system, of which he gives an effective explanation, far superior in breadth to those given by others. He also took care to resolve the criticisms which had been levelled, on the basis of the precise and actual statements of Copernicus, and he pointed out to the judges di Magini and di Clavio the greater exactitude of the calculations made by Copernicus on the basis of his hypotheses. From the pages dedicated to Copernicus there is a very evident preference by Pázmány for the Copernican hypothesis, which apart from other things, is simpler by far than the others. Nor, for him, does the text of Holy Scripture create any obstacle to this notion.[58] There are many commentators on the Bible who, in order to explain its references to the movement of the sun, point to Copernicus; among these Diego da Zuñica deserves special mention. More probably, the little verse 6 of Chapter 9 of the Book of Job alludes to an earthquake, but in any case the theory of the movement of the earth and the immobility of the sun does not contradict Scripture; in fact common parlance habitually attributes to the sun the movement of the earth, since to us it seems that the sun does move, in the same way, as Virgil mentions, as the buildings of a port seem to move when the ship begins to move away from the landing-stage.[59]

The *Commentary on Job* by Diego da Zuñica and that in Pázmány's *De Coelo* witness to a certain trend in the thinking of the church, which saw in Copernicus above all the astronomer who had made the reform of the calendar possible with his calculations – and in this undertaking the whole prestige of the Holy See had been involved. They enable us both to understand the interest which Galileo's theories aroused, and the relative support they gained, and also to take account of the doubts and reservations over the possibility of a straight condemnation of the Copernican system and thus of the attempts made to avoid it.[60] Meanwhile there were two interventions which tried to re-state the "Augustinian/Thomist" line; the first was due to the Carmelite friar Paolo Antonio Foscarini, Provincial of Calabria, and the second to Tommaso Campanella, on the invitation, or so it seems, of Cardinal Caetani, a member of the Congregation for the Index.

In January 1615, Foscarini addressed to Sebastiano Fontone, the General of the Carmelite Order, a letter "[…] concerning the opinion of the Pythagoreans and of Copernicus […] in which there is concord and harmony with the words of Holy Scripture and the theological propositions which can now be adduced against such opinions".[61] The Carmelite in his writing pointed to the true problem which arose with the Copernican theory: the ecclesiastical authorities ran the risk of dragging a matter which belonged to the study of nature into the context of religious doctrine, by presenting it as a question of faith and thus exposing the Church, in a more or less distant future, to a possible refutation on the level of natural science. This would demonstrate without a shadow of doubt the factual error into which it had fallen, and on which the statement of a religious nature would be founded. The Aristotelian/Thomist opinion could not be considered to be true because it was founded on a well-established tradition either from the point of view of philosophical-natural teaching or from the exegetical standpoint, which had acquired such importance as to take the place of certain aspects of the former. Tradition, warned Foscarini, was certainly the sure guide to the truth of the verities of faith, and as such should be followed and upheld, but, as far as concerns the teachings which do not transcend natural matters, and "depend in every thing on sense", and hence on the natural sciences, it was necessary to evaluate with great care, and welcome new theories which offered a more convincing interpretation of natural phenomena, based on reason and the evidence of facts.[62] This was a fair consideration, which appealed to the ecclesiastical authorities to pay careful attention when assessing the matter, and above all to review convictions passively accepted without any serious intellectual commitment. This observation provoked rethinking, and a desire to carry the argument in progress to greater depths. The Archbishop of Pisa, for example, had begun by "recalling Castelli to order", and he had virtually enjoined him to leave aside "certain extravagant opinions, and in particular those on the movement of the earth" […] because these opinions, apart from being nonsense, were dangerous, scandalous and bold, being in direct conflict with Holy Scripture" But after having read Galileo's two letters and then that of Foscarini, he had come to realise the terms of the question and the reasons of the "innovators": […] he no longer says that they are nonsense, but now begins to say that Copernicus was truly a great man and a great genius". This is what Castelli wrote to Galileo.[63]

Cardinal Caetani, too, must have had doubts and rethinkings since he was led to ask for the opinion of a theologian who was not all that "orthodox", though known, and indeed celebrated, for his wide learning. Tommaso

Campanella was still, at this point, imprisoned in Castel dell'Uovo in Naples. His opinion, which was later published in 1622 with the very significant title *Apologia pro Galilaeo*, arrived on the Cardinal's desk seven days after the decision of the Congregation, and it did not serve to uphold the cause of Galileo on that particular occasion; however it certainly witnessed to the continuity of the exegetical tradition which referred specifically to the teachings of St Augustine and St Thomas.[64]

To deal with questions of a religious kind, according to Campanella, it is necessary to possess both divine zeal and science. The former is the guarantee that our enquiry is aimed at the truth and does not become an instrument for achieving other more worldly ends – generally meaning riches and power. But zeal alone is not enough; he insists especially on the importance of scientific knowledge for what concerns the understanding of the Biblical text. The truth, and hence the search for truth, characterises and distinguishes Christianity from the religions of the Classical world, which imposed limits on philosophical and scientific enquiry; they were to accept the divinity as it was defined by the Lawmakers. There could be no conflict between truth and Christianity, as far as Campanella was concerned: "Thus those who claim that the Christian religion should prohibit genuine scientific study and research into the field of physics and astronomy, either have a mistaken conception of Christianity, or lay upon others the pretext for holding them in suspicion. Certainly, if the Christian religion is truly overflowing with all truth, and exempt from any lie, not only does it have nothing to fear from speculation, but finds confirmation in it".[65] Science cannot be reduced to the thoughts of this or that philosopher, to the knowledge of this or that astronomer; nor must we force ourselves to adapt the Bible to one or the other, but we must commit ourselves rather to enquiring with an open mind into nature, which is the work of God, of the wisdom of God: "Our science is nothing but a spark. Knowledge, therefore, can be read in the whole book of God, which is the world, and more and more of it is discovered and this is why the Sacred Scriptures refer us to it and not to the worthless little books of man".66

Thus in the perspective of Christianity seen as the essential premises for a true rationality, open to all scientific enquiry, Campanella stresses the distinction between theology, philosophy and natural science in order to insist on the thesis that the Scriptures must not be considered as texts from which we may derive scientific knowledge, given that they essentially concern the truths of faith: i.e. what pertains to the supernatural reality, the subject of Revelation. And knowledge of this cannot be obtained through mere human rationality: "[…] Neither Holy Moses not the Lord Jesus revealed physics and astronomy to us"; indeed God has left the world to the investigations of men (*Ecclesiastes 3.11)* so that "our mind, through the created world, may understand the invisible things of divinity (*St Paul's Letter to the Romans, Ch.1).* On the contrary, these have taught (us) to live holy lives and to know the supernatural teachings, for which human illumination alone is not enough".67 St Augustine and St Thomas have rightly called the attention of theologians and exegetes to the need to proceed with extreme caution when they make statements or form judgments on the basis of Scripture which concern facts or phenomena which are the subject of the study of philosophy or natural science. For it would be possible to maintain erroneous ideas, which would end by throwing discredit on Christian doctrine, and diminishing the actual authority of Scripture. We must be very careful not to offer the adversaries of Christianity pretexts for facile criticism, since it may come to be regarded as a religion contrary to study and science. In support of these considerations, Campanella quotes passages from *The Confessions* and from *De Genesi ad litteram* by Augustine, and from the *Responsio ad magistrum Ioannem de Vercellis* by Thomas Aquinas, in which as we have already mentioned the problem of the relations between science and scripture were considered.

Attention and caution were also recommended by the fact that St Augustine and St Thomas, like other authoritative church writers, among them Lactantius and Procopius of Gaza, when commenting on the Scriptures, had made a series of statements which subsequent geographical discoveries and the astronomic studies of the modern age had shown, beyond any doubt to be erroneous. Lactantius and St Augustine, for example, maintained that the Antipodes could not exist. And yet navigators have demonstrated that their statement is contrary to the truth; some have said, on the other hand, that in the other hemisphere paradise, or purgatory or hell itself are to be found, as Dante, Isidoro and others held. If these statements corresponded to the "real meaning of Scripture", we would have to conclude with the statement "that the truth now revealed by Columbus would be contrary to, or not in conformity with, divine Scripture".[68] But this is a conclusion that no interpreter would want to uphold: we have, therefore, to explain the biblical text insofar as it refers to natural facts on the basis of the knowledge that has been acquired in the context of philosophy and science.

For all these reasons, it is not correct, according to the teachings of St Augustine and St Thomas, nor is it prudent, after the geographical discoveries of the modern age, to involve Scripture in the Copernican issue, which is not to be defined on the basis of the biblical text. The question posed by Galileo cannot be "closed" by a decision made by the ecclesiastical authorities; it must remain "open" to discussion and to new scientific research. "For these reasons (Campanella warned) if Galileo ends by triumphing, our theologians will have furnished the heretics with no little ammunition against the Catholic faith, because everyone now in Germany and France and England, in Poland, Denmark Sweden, etc., has warmly embraced this theory and the use of the telescope. If, on the other hand, Galileo's thesis were to prove false, no problems at all would arise from it for theology [...] Nor can any charge of falsity be levelled against Galileo, because he is not moving on the basis of mere opinion, but of experimental observations made in the book of the world; nor is he proposing his theory as a matter of faith, with the risk that if it were to be disproved, it would expose both himself and the Bible to ridicule".[69]

7. Cardinal Bellarmine: Science and Hypothesis

The cautious and reserved approach which Campanella recommended, little followed if not completely ignored by the theologians and consultants of his Order, was substantially shared by a sizeable group of cardinals who had followed the discoveries of Galileo with great interest: Francesco Maria Del Monte, Scipione Borghese (the nephew of the Pope), Peretti Montalto, Odoardo Farnese, Maffeo Barberini, Giambattista Dati, Federico Borromeo, Roberto Ubaldini, Pietro Aldobrandini, Alessandro Orsini, Giambattista Bonsi, Luigi D'Este, Giovanni Battista Bandini, Carlo de' Medici, Luigi Capponi, Vincenzo Gonzaga and Bonifacio Caetani. A similar attitude was adopted by the mathematicians and astronomers of the Collegio Romano, and by the most authoritative representative of the Jesuits, Cardinal Robert Bellarmine, who certainly played a leading role in the 1616 trial, along with Maffeo Barberini.

Since 1611, Clavio and his colleagues at the Collegio Romano had been taking an interest, as we mentioned, in the discoveries of Galileo. On the occasion of the astronomic observations which had been made during the visit of the Pisan scientist, Bellarmine had requested the mathematicians of the Jesuit order for information on these discoveries. It may be interesting to note that in their reply, Clavio and his fellow astronomers limited themselves to confirming to Bellarmine what Galileo had maintained in the *Nuncius Sidereus*, without making any references to the consequences, which in some ways were quite obvious, of these discoveries for Aristotelian physics, and for the Aristotelian/Ptolemaic view of the universe.[70] The surface of the moon, the sunspots, the movements of Venus and Mars around the sun, the satellites of Jupiter, all demonstrated that certain essential principles of the Aristotelian notion of the "heavens" could not be upheld, and this in turn brought about a crisis in the actual Aristotelian concept of nature, and a split in that synthesis between Aristotelian philosophy and theology on which the whole ecclesiastical worldview was based. And the Society of Jesus, by its constitution, was supposed to be a guarantor of that world view.

In the latest edition of his commentary on the *Sphaera* of Giovanni di Sacrobosco, which had appeared after 1611, Clavio provided information on the discoveries of Galileo, and let it be clearly understood that a critical revision of the traditional astronomical system was by now required. "Things being so, let the astronomers see how the celestial orbs must be disposed in order that these phenomena can be saved": he would have expressed himself in this way to Galileo during the discussions which he had with him in 1611.[71] Fr. Greinberger, who succeeded Clavio after the latter's death, and was Bellarmine's adviser in 1615-16, did not hide from his fellow Jesuit that he himself was favourably disposed towards the Copernican system, which he would have shared with Clavio himself. It is certain that in May 1615, Monsignor Dini wrote to Galileo: "[…] I understand that many Jesuits in secret are of the same opinion, even though they still remain silent".[72]

This silence, among those who undoubtedly could have spoken in defence of the traditional notion, was really significant, and must have had a certain influence on Bellarmine, in the sense of urging him to seek a solution which would make it possible to take the Copernican theories into consideration, and hence also the arguments of Galileo, while at the same time maintaining the interpretation which had been established on the basis of the correspondence between the geocentric system and the Scriptures. An extremely authoritative expert on Biblical exegesis, he had taken an interest in these very problems without hiding the importance which the scientific discoveries might have in the interpretation of Scripture when it referred to natural phenomena.[73]

Commenting in 1571 on the 69th *quaestio* in the first part of the Summa, in which St Thomas speaks of celestial movements, he had made a reference to the Copernican thesis of the movement of the earth, without, however, pointing out the conflict with the Bible, opining that the interpreter could choose among the various theories put forward by the astronomers that which was most in conformity with Scripture. But he had not omitted to specify that, if in the future a solution was put forward aimed at explaining the text with arguments based on science, "then it will have to be seen how they must understand Scripture in order not to contradict an established truth. And certainly, it is a fact that the true sense of Scripture cannot be in conflict with any other truth, whether philosophical or astronomical".[74]

The new astronomical discoveries, and the interpretation which Galileo gave them, had raised the problem of deciding whether they were matters of "consolidated truth": this was undoubtedly the most delicate aspect of the question, because it was necessary to consider and then judge whether the proofs adduced by Galileo in favour of the Copernican system were such as finally to exclude both the Ptolemaic system and that of Tycho. Now Galileo's theses certainly showed the first to be unfounded, but could also be used to uphold the latter, indeed under certain aspects they seemed actually to confirm it. As historians of the Galileo question have now long recognised, if the scientist succeeded in refuting the arguments against the Copernican system, he was not able, even because of the inadequacy of the scientific instruments available, to give proof positive from the scientific point of view of the movement of the earth.[75] This was the reason, despite the interest in the Copernican theory, for all the caution and reservations; for the doubts on the part of the mathematicians of the Collegio Romano. The situation was substantially that indicated by Canon Quarengo; "[…] and even though the novelty of his opinion is not fully convincing, yet it nevertheless convicts of vanity the majority of the arguments by which his opponents seek to defeat him".

While Galileo's opinion could not be accepted, because it was not sufficiently proven, neither could it be rejected, because it was based on certain new astronomical phenomena. There was, therefore, no other solution than that of resuming the thesis already put forward by Osiander, and considering the new planetary systems as mere "mathematical hypotheses", useful only for resolving problems connected with the calculation of the irregular movement of the planets. From this point of view no conflict existed with Scripture. Bellarmine expressed his opinion in this sense, in a letter dated April 1615 to Fr Foscarini, who had sent him his writings on the Copernican system for the Cardinal's judgment: "I would say that it seems to me that your reverence and Sig Galileo would be prudent to content yourselves with speaking *ex suppositione*, and not in absolute terms, as I have always believed Copernicus to have done. Because to say that supposing the earth moves and the sun is fixed, all the appearances are better preserved than by proposing eccentrices and epicycles, is very well said, and carries no danger whatever, and this is enough for mathematics; but to seek to affirm that the sun is really at the centre of the universe and only revolves on itself without moving from the east to the west, and that the earth is in the third heavenly circle and turns with great velocity round the sun is a very dangerous thing, not only to clash with all the scholastic philosophers and theologians, but also to harm the Holy Faith by rendering the Holy Scriptures false [...]".[76] On the other hand Bellarmine did not hold that it was possible to revise the common opinion of the Fathers as of the modern commentators "about Genesis, about the Psalms, about Ecclesiastes, about Joshua", because everyone in his judgment (but not in fact all the moderns, as we have seen) "agrees in expounding *ad literam* that the sun is in the heavens and revolves around the earth with great velocity, and that the earth is very far from the heavens and is at the centre of the immobile world". Bellarmine thus seems to ignore the thinking of Melchior Cano, who in contrast was favourable to a critical reconsideration of the Fathers on the basis of the new scientific discoveries. The Church, therefore, could not "tolerate" that "Scripture should be given a meaning contrary to the Holy Fathers and all the Greek and Latin commentators".

But this was not the last word: Bellarmine was well aware that a question concerning natural science could not be closed and defined once and for all, on the basis of the authority of Scripture alone. He had already maintained this, as we have seen, in his lectures at Louvain. In replying to Foscarini, he felt it was necessary to specify this point too: and it is certainly the most important part of the letter, in which he notes the concern to find a way of recognising the proper fields of philosophy and natural science. "I say that when there shall be true demonstration that the sun is at the centre of the universe and the earth in the third circle, and that the sun does not circle round the earth but the earth circles round the sun, then it will be necessary to proceed very cautiously in explaining the Scriptures which seem to say the opposite, and rather to say that we do not understand than to say that what is demonstrated is false. But I will not believe that such a demonstration exists until it is plainly shown to me. Nor does this demonstrate that, supposing the sun is at the centre and the earth is in the heavens, the appearances are saved and to demonstrate that in truth the sun is in the centre and the earth in the heavens; because I believe that the former demonstration may exist, but of the second I have the greatest doubt, and in case of doubt we must not leave the Holy Scriptures as expounded by the Holy Fathers".[77]

So Bellarmine does not exclude the possibility that a "true demonstration" of the heliocentric theory may exist; he points out (and he was not mistaken) that it was not yet provided by the proofs put forward by Galileo. In fact, in the state in which "proofs" of the Copernican system stood at that time, it had to be considered as a hypothesis aimed at explaining the apparently irregular movements of the planets, but on from which its correspondence with reality could not be deduced; in the case of "true demonstration" it would certainly have been necessary to revise the traditional interpretation of Scripture in order to understand its real significance. On the basis of these considerations, it became evident that the search for a "true demonstration" was fully legitimate, nor could studies aimed at pursuing it be forbidden. Hence the theory of the hypothetical basis of scientific research and especially researches in astronomy. [78]

This solution, according to Monsignor Dini, was a point in favour of the theses maintained by Galileo, and he referred it to his friend: "[...] in other words that one may write as a mathematician, and by way of hypothesis, as Copernicus wished should be done: although this is not conceded by his followers, it is enough for the others that the same effect results from it": i.e. to allow it to be written about freely, as long as it doesn't "enter into the sacristy" – as we have said previously.[79] But Galileo could not accept this solution: after all, it was his adversaries who had begun the theological dispute, not he himself who was "the first mover of these things: which as far as I am concerned would have been allowed to sleep on"; he had been "pushed" into the sacristy by those who intended to gag him with arguments drawn from Scripture: "[...] they tell me that in these (notions) there are propositions contrary to faith, and I want, as far as I can, to show that perhaps they are deceiving themselves; (but) my lips are sown up and I am ordered not to enter into Scriptural matters". And in fact it was his zeal for the Church which drove him to avoid taking "any resolution which is not totally good, such as declaring that Copernicus did not hold the movement of the earth to be true *in rei natura*, but simply that as an astronomer, he took it for a hypothesis suited to giving reason to appearances, although false in themselves; and that thus it should be allowed that it can be used in this fashion, and may be banned from believing it to be true, which would be, in fact, a declaration of not having read this book".[80]

Now it is just this which is the most important point of the whole debate on the Copernican question: Bellarmine, and after him Maffeo Barberini (as we shall see) when they held that the Copernican thesis was simply a mathematical hypothesis, remained faithful to the Aristotelian distinction between physics and mathematics. This discipline applied to scientific demonstration only within the context of the necessary deductions which could be formulated on the basis of the abstract calculations of quantity and extension. Mathematical truths are such only in reference to the logical proceedings on the basis of which they have been defined, and thus they cannot be transferred to natural reality with the consequence that they do not allow us to know natural phenomena and their mechanisms, knowledge which belongs to the philosophy of nature. On the other hand Copernicus and Galileo (with more mature awareness) had sought to found a new science based on the intimate connection between mathematics and nature – hence the reference to Pythagoras and Plato – capable of substituting Aristotelian physics and producing not a merely 'hypothetical' knowledge, but true knowledge, applicable to natural reality. For Galileo, therefore, it was a matter of better knowledge of and guaranteeing the validity of the results of the research, and this was only possible if the conclusions of the scientific demonstrations had some correspondence with reality: his 'realism' and the rejection of the 'hypothesism' of Bellarmine and Barberini were intimately connected with the new logic of the experimental method, which was based on a positive determination – measurement based on calculation – which could be assumed on the basis of natural reality. Thus to accept the theory of a hypothesis meant for Galileo turning to the old Aristotelian physics which did not permit any satisfactory explanation of the new scientific discoveries. This is perhaps the reason why Galileo, at certain moments of the debate, laid stress on his 'realism', and showed no interest in the value which the hypothesis might have as a scientific conjecture aimed at knowing, and hence at interpreting, the phenomena of nature in experimental fashion, defining the context of our scientific knowledge. The theory of the hypothesis was not put forward by Bellarmine or by Barberini as a logical premise of experimental research which would lead to a true conclusion: it seemed to find confirmation, even in the way in which it had been formulated, in the fact that Galileo had not succeeded in giving scientific proofs which would confirm the heliocentric thesis in incontrovertible fashion. Fr Grienberger, who considered the Copernican system to be of great interest, had noted that Galileo's arguments seemed "more plausible than true".[81]

8. Cardinal Barberini and Galileo

As already mentioned, Maffeo Barberini too was following the controversy aroused by the denunciations of Lorini and Caccini with the greatest interest. He had met Galileo in Rome in 1611, and had been very careful to see that he was informed on the results of his researches. He had supported the scientist's theory on the occasion of a discussion about the floating of solids, which had taken place in September of that year, at the court of Cosimo II; he had been informed by Galileo himself in June 1612, of the polemics concerning sunspots. He had such esteem for him that he had later praised his astronomic discoveries in an Alcaic ode.[82]

Maffeo Barberini was aware of the particularly embarrassing situation, so to speak, in which the church authorities found themselves as a result of the Copernican dispute. It was known to all that *De revolutionibus* had been published as a result of the strong insistence of some influential churchmen, and that Paul III had accepted its dedication, as of a work which was fully in conformity to the principles of Catholicism; that those who had worked on the reform of the calendar had made constant reference to *De revolutionibus*; there were doctrines which in certain respects had received the approval of three popes: Clement VII, Paul III and Gregory XIII – especially Paul III, who had reconstituted that Inquisition which was now preparing to judge the *De Revolutionibus* – had not considered of great importance the question of its relations with Scripture, explicitly pointed out by Copernicus in the dedication. There was a clear contradiction between the previous attitude of favour and approval, and that of condemnation which was taking shape. Galileo, naturally, made no bones about pointing this out: "[…] and while I follow the teaching of a book accepted by Holy Church, philosophers completely devoid of any such doctrines come out against me and say that in them (the writings) there are propositions against the faith…".[83] This explains an attitude of caution in Curia circles, which had followed the question more closely, and a certain tendency to raise the tone of the discussion to see whether the matter couldn't be closed in the investigatory stage. The theory of the hypothesis was, as far as Barberini was concerned, the condition for achieving such an aim, and he let it be known through Ciampoli to Galileo: "Signor Cardinal Barberini, who as you know from experience, has always admired your qualities, said to me yesterday evening that he would appreciate greater caution in this issue, to avoid going beyond the reasonings of Ptolemy or Copernicus, or finally that you should not pass beyond the limits of physics or mathematics, because the theologians claim that interpreting Scripture is their prerogative […].[84] This question was further discussed between the Cardinal and Galileo, very probably as a result of the discussions held at the home of Lorenzo Magalotti – who later became a cardinal under Urban VIII (Maffeo Barberini). In these discussions, Francesco Ingoli among others took part, the secretary of the Congregation for Spread of the Faith, in defence of the geo-centric system.[85] The record of the discussion, which must have been very profound, has been left us by Fr Agostino Oreggi, who was also later to be nominated Cardinal by Urban VIII and was to take part in the Commission which judged Galileo in 1633.[86]

According to what Oreggi tells us, the discussion did not confine itself to the problem of the relationship between the heliocentric theory and Holy Scripture; the question of interpretation of the Scriptures must have been a mere premise, though an important one, for examining a delicate theological problem, that of the relationship between God and nature, in the light of the arguments that Galileo had adduced in defence of the Copernican system, and hence of the new conception of science that Galileo was professing. If the structure of nature corresponded to mathematical and geometrical relations (the great book of nature is written in mathematical and geometrical characters, the scientist was later to say in the *Saggiatore*), from which the laws which regulate natural phenomena are to be deduced, and if these, as such, take on the character of necessity, and cannot be otherwise, nature thus conceived is seen to be a substantial limit on the infinite power and freedom of God, who would end up by being placed under necessity by nature itself, and by becoming identified with it.[87] If on the other hand it is intended to maintain the distinction between God and nature, and hence between the supernatural and the natural, it is essential to hold firmly to the absolute freedom and power of God in the face of nature, with the consequence that the arrangement of the planets as envisaged by Copernicus is one of the ways in which the astronomic phenomena which we study may be produced, but not the sole way, because many others could also exist, which cannot be envisaged by human reason. In order to affirm that it is the only way, we must demonstrate that the other possible ways are contradictory. We must prove, in other words that God would have contradicted himself if he had created the Universe in any way other than that indicated by the Copernican system. Such a demonstration cannot be provided, because the series of possibilities in nature cannot be envisaged or "exhausted" by human reason. This is why, according to Maffeo Barberini, no true test of the Copernican theory could ever be made, which responds in everything and in all respects to natural reality, but only a hypothetical one, from which it was not legitimate to deduce any definitive conclusion concerning this issue.[88]

Galileo did not reply to the Cardinal's objection; he remained silent: possibly he felt it was irrelevant as far as the logic of his arguments was concerned, and thus he didn't understand the connection with the new form of science that he was proposing. Nor did he succeed in resolving the problem during the discussions which he had between 1624 and 1630 with Barberini, by this time Pope Urban VIII. He thus gave the impression to his illustrious interlocutor, either then or later, that he had implicitly accepted the theory of the hypothesis. On the other hand, Barberini, solely concerned with measuring Galileo's theories against the essential principles of the theological notion of God, ended by losing sight of the possibilities of determined and detailed truths, which arose out of the natural science propounded by Galileo, and became convinced that the only truth was that which was expressed at the level of logic and philosophy, of which it was essential to give the required demonstration.

If we want to understand the motives which explain the mutual incomprehension between Maffeo Barberini and Galileo, and the doubts to which it gave rise, we should remember that the scientist insisted that he was "the mathematician and philosopher" of the Grand Duke, and laid the greatest importance on the intimate connection between the two disciplines, since his programme was one of devising a natural science which would be capable of completely taking the place of Aristotelian natural philosophy. Before taking up his position with the Grand Duke, he had been careful to specify: "[...] I wish that in addition to the title of mathematician, your Highness would add that of philosopher, as I may claim to have studied philosophy for more years than I have spent months pure mathematics".[89] In this perspective, i.e. in the close interconnection of philosophy and natural science, he had stressed in a letter to Marco Welser on sunspots, the difference which existed between pure astronomers, who formed mere hypotheses aimed solely at calculating the movements of the planets, and at "saving the phenomena", and philosophic astronomers who instead aimed to discover the reality of nature in its truth, and "seek to investigate, as their greatest and most wondrous problem, the true constitution of the universe, since this constitution is, and in one way only, true reality, impossible to be of any other nature, and because of its greatness and nobility is worthy to be placed ahead of any other question discoverable by speculative genius".[90] And again, in a letter to Monsignor Dini in March 1615, he had pointed out that Copernicus had certainly, "as far as saving the appearances was concerned… already made much effort earlier on", but then "donning the robes of a philosopher", he had set himself the problem of the real constitution of the universe "knowing that if a partial feigned disposition, and one that was not true, could satisfy the appearances, much more would have been obtained from that which was true and real, and at the same time there would have been such an excellent gain in knowledge to philosophy such as is the knowledge of the true disposition of the parts of the universe […].[91]

In the discussions with his opponents, Galileo had thus stressed with particular insistence between 1612 and 1616 the intimate connection existing between the new science and philosophy, which made it possible to arrive at the knowledge of the "true constitution of the universe", "unique, and impossible that it should be otherwise". After these statements, which he would certainly have made during his discussion with Barberini, it was inevitable that the question was taken up on a theological plane, to investigate the relationship between God and nature, as they emerged from the arguments of Galileo. Maffeo Barberini did nothing but continue the dialogue with Galileo, bringing to its final consequences the theory that science was in a position to know the real organisation of the universe, and demonstrating the contrary nature of the assumption. In substance he took note of, and criticised, a new direction in philosophy, intimately connected with modern science; the "scientism" which surpassed the limits of experimental science and ended by turning itself into a philosophy. Galileo, in fact, showed no signs of awareness of the problem; he was not conscious that in the way that he was presenting the truth of the new science, there was a "philosophical response" which at other moments in his discourse he had, and would have continued to, reject. Experimental science is not knowledge of everything (the true system of the universe) but of its individual parts, of certain phenomena in their quantitative aspects. He, on the other hand, continued to assert the experimental truth of the system, or of the composition of the universe, as an all-embracing synthesis of nature, thus directly calling both theology and religion into question, since they (justly) wished to maintain the distinction between science and nature. On the other hand, Maffeo Barberini, although he had grasped the problem of the philosophical and epistemological basis of the new science, by warning of the limits inherent in his own method, he ended up by considering the truth exclusively in the perspective of logic and philosophy, and denying the experimental truth – reduced to mere abstractions – hypotheses – the correspondence of which to reality could never be proved.

Maffeo Barberini continued to the end to choose the path of pragmatism. The scientist could continue his work, and indeed he should be encouraged so that science could produce hypotheses which were useful to the community. On the basis of the *De revolutionibus,* in fact, it had been possible to reform the calendar; the abstractions which it led to were intellectual instruments which could provide notable services to human activity. It would, for example, be possible to resolve the problem of determining the longitude during the course of navigation, by making use of astronomic calculation to set the route with certainty. There was a need, in conclusion, to proceed with cautious wisdom, to reaffirm the authority of Scripture, but not to condemn science, free to carry out its activities in the context of the hypotheses which it formulated. This was the conviction of Maffeo Barberini, to which he would later give effect in his judgment before the Congregation of the Holy Office, and in the decision of the Congregation of the Index regarding the works of Copernicus.

9. The decree of the Congregation of the Index in 1616, and the condemnation of the heliocentric system

As we have seen, Galileo had not grasped the full value of the argument put forward by Cardinal Barberini: to reject and affirm the truth of the Copernican system was all one to him, with saying that what he had seen and 'discovered' with the telescope was not true. Accepting the "theory of the hypothesis" meant turning to reasoning with the principles and the concepts of Aristotelian natural philosophy. He continued to assert the truth of the heliocentric system. In fact, he believed that he had identified the physical proof of the movement of the earth in the phenomenon of the tides; he wrote about this to Cardinal Alessandro Orsini,[92] who, since was convinced of the rightness of the scientist's arguments, decided to intervene directly with the Pope, in order to call his attention to the appropriateness of favourable consideration of the theories upheld by Galileo. But Paul V, in contrast to his predecessor Paul III, had no interest in scientific issues, and in astronomy in particular. He was a jurist, with a specialised knowledge of canon law, and was above all concerned with defending traditional theological opinions. If we are to believe the Ambassador of Tuscany, he was suspicious of curiosity and of the "ferments" of the philosophical and literary worlds, as he was of the novelties which arose in them.

In the Consistory of 24th February 1616, Cardinal Orsini had a chance to speak in favour of Galileo, but he obtained a negative result, as Guicciardini feared: "[…] I do not know how considerately and prudently he spoke to the Pope in recommending this Galileo. The Pope told him that it was better that he should persuade him to set aside this opinion. Orsini gave some sort of an answer, pressing the Pope, who cut off the discussion and told him he would remand the whole negotiation to the Lord Cardinals of the Holy Office. And when Orsini had left, His Holiness caused Bellarmine to be recalled to him, and talked about this matter; they concluded that this opinion of Galileo's was erroneous and heretical, and the day before yesterday I hear that they called together a Congregation on this issue […]".93 The ambassador's information was not completely correct, and as he was irritated by Galileo's "propaganda" in favour of the heliocentric theory – which he considered inopportune and counterproductive (as indeed in some ways it was) – he had not bothered to gather information on the modifications which, at the last minute, it had been thought appropriate to apply to the decision to condemn.

Just at that time, Maffeo Barberini intervened, in agreement with Bellarmine, to prevent an explicit declaration of heresy against the Copernican system, and to avoid the work *De revolutionibus* being completely prohibited, but only 'amended' in those expressions from which it was possible to assume that the heliocentric theory had been upheld as a "natural truth". In 1628 he declared to Campanella that if it had depended on him, it would not have come to a condemnation of the Copernican system. By a decree of 5th March 1616, the Congregation of the Index, while it declared the ancient Pythagorean doctrine, recently resumed by Copernicus, to be contrary to Scripture, completely banned the writing of Fr Foscarini, forbade the reading of the *Commentary on Job* of Diego da Zuñica, and of the *De revolutionibus* of Copernicus, until provision had been made to correct the expressions in which the movement of the earth around the sun was upheld.[94]

As is well known, the correction of Copernicus' work lasted four years: in the Warning for the amendment of the *De revolutionibus,* the justification for the provision was given: after noting that the prohibition was determined by the fact that the heliocentric theory was not considered a hypothesis but rather a natural truth ("non per hypothesim tractare sed ut verissima adstruere") it was specified that nevertheless the work of Copernicus had been permitted because it provided particularly useful knowledge to society ("*quia in iis multa sunt reipublicae utilissima*"): the reform of the Gregorian Calendar was just one proof of this.[95]

The Copernican issue, and hence that of Galileo too, had been taken up, therefore, in the context of the logic of reasons of State: the principle of the truth of the Scriptures was reasserted, and thus the condemnation of the heliocentric system was pronounced. But the *utilitas reipublicae* imposed an exception or a limit on the condemnation, and the related prohibitions. The possibility must be acknowledged for natural science to continue its work of research, from which useful results for the community could be expected. The importance of science for the purposes of *respublica* did not escape the attention of those who framed the Monito: Maffeo Barberini and Bellarmine. An essentially 'diplomatic' solution was proposed, therefore, recognising at one and the same time the needs connected to the traditional interpretation of Scripture in order to re-affirm the truth and the "*libertas philosophandi in naturalibus*" in the context of a hypothesis assumed for the study of natural phenomena. The intention was to guarantee science a space for itself, which was defined by the hypothesis, as long as this did not go beyond its limits, and did not enter into the field proper to theology and philosophy. An implicit recommendation to the scientist was formulated, which might be expressed in the famous phrase of Manzoni, "*adelante con judicio*".

Thus, if it was held necessary to pronounce a condemnation against the heliocentric theory for the purposes of the interpretation of Scripture, this did not in itself open the way for a denunciation against Galileo. The process was closed in the investigative stage. Paul V ruled that it should be limited to communicating the decision of the Congregation of the Index to the scientist, so that he should give his assent in due form. On 26th February 1616, Cardinal Bellarmine called Galileo to his palace, and in the presence of four ecclesiastics, among whom was the commissioner of the Congregation of the Holy Office, the Dominican father Segizzi, he notified him of the decision of the Index, and admonished him to be obedient to it.[96]

Given Galileo's submissive attitude and the particular favour in which he himself was held, did they limit themselves to the simple admonition, or did they, immediately afterwards, despite his acceptance, notify him of the Precept, a formal act by which he was to undertake not to hold or to teach (obligations deriving from the admonition) and not to deal in any way with the Copernican thesis, otherwise he would incur the condemnation of the Holy Office? This question touches one of the most delicate points of the whole matter of the trials of 1616 and 1633. As is known, in the manuscript of the trial preserved in the

Secret Archives of the Vatican, the original version of the Precept is missing, and in its place is a page containing the formula of the Precept without the prescribed formularies; i.e. without the signature of a notary, of Galileo's witnesses. A document in other words of no value whatsoever from the standpoint of due process of law. The Precept, therefore, was not intimated, and the surviving page is nothing more than an "annotation" prepared by the notary in anticipation of the summoning of Galileo, but which was not then made use of, and was not subscribed; it remained, however, among the papers of the trial.[97]

In the declaration made by Bellarmine to the Congregation on the results of the summoning of the scientist, some reference is made to the Precept, indeed it is stated that Galileo immediately showed his assent.[98] Bellarmine then informed the Pope that Galileo had accepted the decision of the Index, without making any objection, and after a few days Paul V received him in audience, conversing with him for three quarters of an hour. During the discussion, according to what the scientist himself tells us, "my resolution was approved with many and repeated praises. I gave his Holiness to understand the malignancy of my persecutors and some of their false calumnies; and here he replied to me that my integrity and sincerity of mind had also been recognised by him […] and before I left, he repeated to me many times that he was well-disposed to me and showed me, too, with great affection, on all occasions, his good disposition in my favour".[99]

It seems difficult to believe that the Pope would have granted an audience, and then expressed himself in those terms, to a person – certainly an illustrious one and under the protection of the Grand Duke – who had been served with a Precept, a provision of a certain seriousness which presupposed a refusal of assent on the part of the scientist. Nor can we imagine that Bellarmine would not have informed the Pope of the Precept, information which would in any case have been supplied to him by the Commissioner of the Holy Office. But there is a final testimony, of special significance, in which no mention is made of the Precept; this is the declaration issued, on Galileo's request, by Bellarmine in which he testifies that the scientist had not been constrained to any kind of abjurement, not had he suffered any punishment for his opinions, but he had simply had communicated to him the censure relating to the Copernican thesis.[100]

The question aroused by the heliocentric theory thus seemed decided, but the logic of "raison d'état" notoriously does not provide definitive and unchangeable solutions; instead it suggests exceptions and modifications of the general rules according to the situations, in view of the *utilitas reipublicae:* thus it indicates contingent solutions which can be modified or revised. This was precisely the underlying intention of Galileo, after he had given his assent to the decision of the ecclesiastical authorities. As mathematician and philosopher of the Grand Duke, he knew and recognised the supreme reasons of the prince which must be obeyed: "[…] for I know how much it behoves me to obey and believe the decisions of (my) superiors, as those which have been gathered from higher knowledge to which the low state of my ingenuity in itself may not arrive". But this did not mean that it was not permitted to him to utter, with the same excuse of "raison d'état", his true opinion and intention, which he had never renounced. Two years later, in fact, in 1618, he sent to the Archduke Leopold of Austria the *Lettere solari* and the *Discorso sulle maree*, in which he sought to demonstrate the movement of the earth, and that after ecclesiastical censure, described as "fantasy, chimers, poetry and dream" - a dream, he let it be understood clearly, that had become the very reason for the existence of his life as a scientist.[101]

SECTION 2

II. THE 1633 TRIAL

1. The dispute over the comets: Galileo, The Collegio Romano and Orazio Grassi

After the publication of the Decree of the Congregation of the Index (5th March 1616), Galileo retreated into a strict silence, as far as the Copernican question was concerned. But "the heavens", it seems appropriate to say, had willed otherwise. In 1618, three comets appeared, the last of which was particularly splendid. They were situated in the constellation of Scorpio; naturally, these heavenly phenomena aroused the greatest excitement in public opinion, always ready to comment on the unusual "portents" in the skies, and also in the scientific world, among the mathematicians and astronomers. Galileo's young pupil Virginio Cesarini wrote to him about them; he had been greatly struck by the scientist during his last stay in Rome, and he had had an opportunity to view the comets in Rome in a "most clear sky" and "revealed by a powerful sunset": "The novel things seen in these past days in the skies awaken even incurious men, and compel the sleepiest and laziest people in Rome to rise from their beds, so that you cannot imagine what excitement the appearance of two comets has aroused, and what ludicrous and commonplace opinions they have given rise to". He sent Galileo a report on his observations, accompanied by a "professional opinion" from the mathematicians of the Collegio Romano, with whom he had had an opportunity to discuss the heavenly phenomena. He asked the scientist to let him know his opinion on the matter.[102]

Another request for clarification and for an opinion came to Galileo a fortnight or so later from Paris, from the court of the King of France (Louis XIII). Domenico Bonsi informed him that in the discussions among the mathematicians about the appearance of the comets, "it was commonly agreed that no one other than your good self could make observations about them, since you had perfect information on similar matters, and because of the good quality of your telescope, since the Grand Duke has excellent instruments for making such observations". He therefore begged Galileo to "satisfy public expectation and curiosity", possibly by a written statement dedicated to his observations and thoughts on the comets.[103] And yet another authoritative figure requested clarification from Galileo, the Archduke Leopold of Austria, who happened to be in Florence and had tried to seek out the scientist, who was then unable to move because of strong and painful attacks of arthritis.[104]

Meanwhile, while Galileo, besieged by so many requests, began to draw up his observations, the mathematicians of the Collegio Romano in Rome were holding an academic meeting, in the course of which Father Orazio Grassi gave a lecture, later published, in which he resumed, and backed up with new arguments, the theories of Tycho Brahe, formulated on the occasion of the comet of 1577. This was a heavenly body, very distant from the moon, with its own orbit around the sun.[105] But the remarks on the comet had a special interest, above all because of the consequences which could be drawn from them about the notion of the planetary system. In fact, the great Danish astronomer, was led to conclude that the earth was immobile at the centre of the planetary system with the planets revolving around the sun and the sun, in turn, revolving around the earth. This was based on the fact that no halts or retrograde movements had been noted in them, which they would have had to show if the earth moved around the sun. Defending and demonstrating the theory of Tycho Brahe on the comets therefore meant putting forward and defending the argument by which the astronomer had rejected the Copernican system and had instead proposed a new kind of geo-centralism.

In this way, the discussion and the polemic on the Copernican system was resumed, even though indirectly. Giulio Rinuccini took the opportunity of recalling Galileo's attention to the "ultimate aims" which had been proposed for the academic gathering held at the Collegio Romano: "The Jesuits made a public Problema of it, which has been printed, and they hold firmly that it is in the heavens, and some of those outside the Jesuit order have spread word that this brings the system of Copernicus to the ground, and that he has no greater contrary argument than this: thus if I were to say to you that it seems to me a thousand years away from knowing his opinion, I believe he will pardon me".[106]

Pleaded with by his friends, and by people in authoritative positions, moved by the sentiment of wanting to live up to the expectations aroused by his fame as a scientist at international level, Galileo, when he had learned of Grassi's lecture, thought it would be appropriate to reveal his own considerations by means of a *Discourse*, inspired and mostly written by him, which was presented by one of his pupils, Mario Guiducci, to the Florentine Academy.[107] In this, after examining the (so to speak) traditional hypotheses, formulated by Pythagoras and Aristotle, and those of the modern astronomers, notably Tycho Brahe and Grassi, he defended the notion of Pythagoras – that the comet was a mere effect of the refraction of solar rays – presenting it with a series of considerations which often stressed the lack of consistency in the arguments put forward by Grassi and accepted by the mathematicians of the Collegio Romano. Since the comet seemed to be a mere illusion, and not a heavenly body, the implicit consequence was that the arguments of Tycho Brahe against the Copernican system were devoid of foundation. In the *Discourse* there is no lack of polemical stabs at the methods and scientific attitudes advanced by Grassi, and by the mathematicians of the Collegio Romano, almost as if he was seeking to bring back into view, sometimes with ironic remarks and expressions, the lack of foundation of the notions upheld by the supporters of Tycho's system.[108]

Galileo thus began a polemic in which he involved the authority and prestige of the highest scientific institution of the Jesuits, which was to have a negative effect on his relations with the Jesuit mathematicians and astronomers. This in turn led to a counter-polemic: in July 1619, Giovanni Ciampoli, after expressing his admiration for the new work, was careful to make a sharp point with the scientist, specifically because of the negative consequences of his untimely, and in certain senses unjustified, attack: "Since you ask me freely, I will readily say to you something which is unlikely to please, and it is that you want to take up swords with the Collegio Romano, in which there has been such public profession of honour towards you. The Jesuits consider themselves greatly offended, and are preparing to reply; and while on this side I am well aware of the soundness of your conclusions, even so I am sorry that there has been such a drop in their benevolence and the applause which they once gave to your name".[109] The scientific debate thus began to be transformed, in certain ways, into a finicky scientific debate.

The *Discourse on the Comet* appeared in Florence around the beginning of June 1619. Fr Grassi, like other scholars from the Collegio Romano, lost no time in identifying it as the work of Galileo, and they did not hide their dismay at such a sharp criticism, which seemed to strike at the authority and prestige of their institution. They needed to reply, therefore, and to defend the scientific credibility of the studies which were taking place at the Collegio Romano. The discussion, which had begun between the two mathematicians and the astronomers, thus assumed after the first exchanges, the tone of a clear and polemical clash, from which inevitably suspicions, jealousy and resentment were to arise and play their part on the occasion of the trial of 1633.

The reply to the *Discourse* was not long in coming. In October 1619, Grassi published in Perugia, under the pseudonym of Lotario Sarsi Sigensano, a work entitled *Libra astronomica ac philosophica*,[110] in which Galileo was challenged directly in the form of a very detailed discussion of the proofs which had been adduced in support of Tycho Brahe's thesis: naturally there was no lack of sharp rebukes against his adversary. For Ciampoli, who wrote to Galileo about it in December 1619, "your writing [seemed] so glorious, and with so many cutting jests".[111] The *Libra Astronomica* of course aroused in turn an indignant reaction among Galileo's friends, members of the Accademia dei Lincei and others, who hastened to write to him, exhorting him to give a satisfactory reply to his critic: the scientist certainly didn't need any exhortations to give yet another demonstration of his "dialectical" capacities, and to demonstrate the errors of his opponent, with that subtle irony which at times assumed a tone of pungent sarcasm. According to some people, it was necessary to provide a critically convincing reply, but without involving the fathers of the Collegio Romano in the polemics, "because" (as Francesco Stelluti noted) "otherwise the whole thing will be unending squabble with those Fathers, who, being so many, take up matters with the whole world and then, if they are in the wrong, want to prove that they aren't. And it can't do us any good to, and indeed may do harm, since they are in particular no friends to new ideas, as indeed all the peripatetics are". Others, on the other hand, held that it was necessary to seize the occasion to "re-dimension" the scientific and cultural prestige of the Order: "[...] and it is very necessary (wrote Giovanni Faber, the Chancellor of the Lincei), to lower the pride of those who believe that all those who aim at any sort of perfection must pass through their school, as from the Trojan Horse".[112]

Meanwhile Galileo, after receiving Sarsi's book, had set to work, and between 1620 and June 1621 he wrote a reply, to which he gave the title *Saggiatore*, to indicate the scrupulousness and attention with which he had weighed up the arguments of his critic. This is certainly one of his finest works, both from the literary point of view and because of the explanation of the criteria on which his method of scientific enquiry was based. To Grassi's prolix arguments based on the appeal to "authority" and his frequent learned quotations, Galileo opposed a logic which began with the convictions acquired through a direct study of phenomena, always related to experiments, which had to be demonstrated through geometry and mathematics, which is the true key for interpreting natural phenomena. Thus in many ways *Il Saggiatore* became the "manifesto" of the new experimental science, and above all of the basic cultural trend which lay behind it; of the "new opinions" as opposed to scholastic Aristotelianism. But at the level of scientific reasoning, in some ways quite positive with regard to the specific question – the nature of the comet – Galileo, as we have noted, paid a very high price:[113] certainly an innovator in the matter of method, had turned himself into a defender, in the question of the comet, of a traditional opinion – which did not correspond to natural truth – maintained by Aristotle; denying the existence of the comet which was seen as a mere astronomic illusion, he had been forced as a result to deny the observations made by Tycho Brahe, the greatest astronomer of the century, and the final proof by Grassi, who was certainly no genius like Galileo, but as a mathematician knew what he was talking about.. In this way they had all headed down a dead-end lane, which had forced them into a series of contradictions, of "errors" of the type of which he was accustomed to accuse his opponents.

In effect his mind was not so much concentrated on the comet - which, moreover, he had not been able to observe because of the illness which had confined him to his bed, while Tycho had dedicated a very careful and detailed study to the argument - as to the logic of the new method of scientific enquiry, which in his mind was all one with the demonstration of the Copernican system. The discussion on the comet, as we have seen, was not interesting in itself but because of the consequences which could be derived from it for the notion of the planetary system.

Both Grassi and Galileo were well aware of the basic question: the former had in fact not failed to mention mischievously in his *Libra* that the *Discourse on the Comet* in effect presupposed the Copernican thesis, which had recently been censured.[114] This observation was clearly intended to cause difficulties for Galileo, but by introducing into the scientific discussion an element of judgment belonging to a different range of considerations, ended by falsifying the scientific debate and boomeranging on the proponent himself. Galileo thus had a chance to put forward once again the need to have an adequately certain knowledge of the planetary system, which it did not seem possible could be attained: "Then, as to the hypothesis of Copernicus, when, for the benefit of us Catholics, we were not brought out of error by more sovereign knowledge, and our blindness illuminated, I do not think that such grace and benefit could have been obtained from the reasons and experiments put forward by Tycho. Since, therefore, the two systems are both false, and that of Tycho is null, Sarsi should not reproach me if, like Seneca, I desire to know the real constitution of the universe. And certainly that demand is great, and very wished for by me, but not amid reproaches and tears do I deplore, as Sarsi says, the "poverty and calamity of this century [...]".[115] While pretending to submit to the ecclesiastical censure, Galileo could not resist accepting it with the pungent irony of a courtier who, along with his praise and flattery, shows up the incongruity and limits of the claim to power. And in this way he seizes the opportunity to stress the stalemate in which astronomic studies are to be found as a result of this very censure.

2. *Urban VIII and Galileo's theories: the* Saggiatore *and the* Letter to Ingoli

Galileo had barely finished writing his *Saggiatore* when a completely unexpected and exceptional event reawakened the hope, in him and his friends, of being able to re-open the question which seemed to have been closed with the condemnation of 1616. On 8th July 1623, Gregory XV died, and in the conclave of 6th August in the same year, Maffeo Barberini was elected Pope. During the intervening years he had written an ode of praise to the discoveries and genius of the scientist.[116] Never had an event seemed to augur so well for the friends of the new opinions: the new Pope began his pontificate while the printing of the *Saggiatore* was in progress; written in the form of a letter to Msgr Virginio Cesarini, the private Chamberlain of Gregory XV, and now Master of the Pope's Chamber, it was published by the Accademia dei Lincei. The work could hardly be otherwise dedicated and presented than to Urban VIII, as a testimony of the extremely high hopes which were reposed in his work as Pontiff. "As a sign of our devotion and a tribute of our genuine service, we bring to You the Saggiatore of our Galileo, of the Florentine discoverer not of new earths, but of no longer seen parts of the heavens [...] We dedicate and offer it to your Holiness, as to one who has a spirit full of true ornaments and splendours, and has a mind turned towards the highest undertakings; desiring that this reasoning on unusual facets of the heavens may be a sign to you of that lively and ardent affection which we feel, to serve and merit the grace of Your Holiness".[117]

Among the Pope's closest associates there were very faithful friends of Galileo; apart from Virginio Cesarini, we also find Monsignor Giovanni Ciampoli, who had been nominated Secretary for the Briefs, and thus had the responsibility for the Pope's official correspondence. He immediately informed Galileo of the success which *Il Saggiatore* had enjoyed with the pope: "[...] it has arisen into such favour with Our Lord the Pope that he has caused it to be read at table" wrote Cesarini; and Ciampoli, in turn, let him know that "having read certain papers to His Holiness, they have pleased him greatly".[118] In this climate of enthusiasm the suggestion arose that Galileo should give new proofs of his great ingenuity, and give full expression to his scientific meditations of these years; his "hidden thoughts"; "Here it is highly desired that there should be some other novelty from your inventiveness: so if you were to resolve to have printed those concepts which have so far remained closed in your mind, I am quite sure that they would get a gracious reception from Our Lord also, for he does not cease to admire your eminence in all things, and to preserve intact the affection he showed you in time past".[119] It seemed to Galileo, therefore, that the right moment had come to resume, directly with the Pope, the question which was so close to his heart, and the occasion was provided by the new visit to Rome in order to render homage to the Pope who was showing so much good will towards him. It is Galileo himself who tells us that Urban VIII granted him as many as six audiences: "As for things here, I have initially received very great honours and favours from Our Lord the Pope, having been as many as six times in long discussions with His Holiness".[120] Unfortunately, the scientist does not provide us with any more detailed accounts of these meetings.

The long discussions that took place with Urban VIII certainly refer to the problems posed by the Copernican thesis, and the relative ecclesiastical censure. They would have enabled Galileo to appreciate that the Pope was still very interested in the question, so that the censure should not be interpreted as an absolute ban on dealing with the question *quoquo modo*. Indeed, the very fact that the Pope had conversed with him for so long seemed to admit the possibility of an eventual re-examination of the condemnation, which was founded first of all on the assertion that the thesis of Copernicus was "philosophically absurd". Now the specific reasons why "in philosophical terms" in the context of human reason and thus of the considerations of mathematicians and astronomers showed that the claimed absurdity of Copernicus' theories could be evaluated with closer attention, and they could be shown to be legitimate. Galileo took advantage of his stay in Rome to establish new and fruitful relations with influential persons in the Curia, in order to call their attention to the importance of the Copernican question, the condemnation of which notably limited the possibilities of proselytism among the protestant nobles and intellectuals, many of whom had been unfavourably impressed by the ecclesiastical censure.

On this occasion Galileo had the possibility of meeting the Dominican Nicolò Riccardi,[121] who was later to be a leading figure in the events which ended in the second trial.

He also met the German humanist, Gaspare Scioppio, well-accepted in German Catholic circles, and the Cardinals of Santa Susanna, Boncompagni and Zollern, who were to intervene with Urban VIII, with special reference to the Copernican question. Galileo's correspondence gives us an interesting insight into these encounters.[122] A week later it was Galileo himself who told Cesi of the outcome of his Roman conversations, of the long discussions he had had with the Pope, of how the initiative to recall the attention of Urban VIII to the controversy over Copernicus had obtained substantial support from Cardinal Zollern.[123] It seemed to Galileo, therefore, that he had got some notable results out of his stay in Rome. There was no "absolute" condemnation of the Copernican theory; it did not enter the field of heretical opinions, but only those that were deemed "bold". In other words, those which conflicted with a constant interpretation of Scripture, and seemed to cast doubt upon the truth of a statement which referred to a natural phenomenon of an experience shared in common by all humanity, which must be received with due caution – in other words as a mere hypothesis aimed at explaining a series of astronomical phenomena. But this did not stop it being taken up again and further pursued on the scientific plane, (i.e. within the context of natural reason), to demonstrate that its alleged absurdity was unfounded, and to clarify, if nothing else, the arguments which made it possible to assume it as a hypothesis which explained the astronomic phenomena, and as such was certainly not something to be considered "an absurdity in philosophy and false in theology". The contexts of natural reason and faith, by a constant tradition, which referred back to St Thomas, were distinct. And in this sense, the Dominican Nicolò Riccardi, like the humanist Gaspare Scioppio, held that astronomic questions did not constitute "matter of faith", and that consequently there was no reason to refer them to the authority of Scripture. These were authoritative opinions of persons of high standing in the life of the Church and of Roman culture, from which it could be understood that there was 'space' to continue a discussion which seemed to have been closed by the censure of 1616.

In the course of his conversations during his third visit to Rome, Galileo was considering the idea of resuming his studies on the Copernican system in an organic way. He and his friends had realised that the situation had changed since the one that had arisen after the 1616 condemnation, and that this was undoubtedly due to the new Pope and to the interest and esteem which he showed towards the scientist and his work. Paul V, as we have seen, had cut short Cardinal Orsini's elocution, in which he defended Galileo. Urban VIII, on the other hand, reminded Cardinal Zoller of the initiative he had taken to modify the condemnation, as if he meant to disown the responsibility for that provision. This response could only be interpreted as a readiness to reconsider the problems raised by the censure of 1616.

The first thing to be done was to refute the arguments adopted in 1616 by one of the defenders of the Ptolemaic system, Francesco Ingoli, the Secretary of the Congregation of Propaganda Fide. He had written a report on the issue in which the question was dealt with both from the scientific and theological viewpoints: *De situ et quiete terrae contra Copernici systema disputatio ad doctissimum mathematicum D. Galilaeum Galilaeum.* Because of the censure which had been imposed, Galileo could not reply, of course, and his silence was interpreted as an acceptance of the arguments put forward by his opponents, or as proof that he had not succeeded in formulating a convincing critique of them. This observation had already been made by Urban VIII himself, in one of the "long discussions" in which the most significant aspects of the Copernican question had evidently been considered.[124]

It was necessary, then, to clear up the doubt which had arisen, and to make known to friends and scholars the essential scientific arguments which worked in favour of the Copernican thesis. It was also necessary to indicate the reasons why the Ptolemaic system could no longer be maintained: thus as soon as he returned to Florence, he wrote the *Letter to Ingoli*,[125] in which the arguments that had been adopted to support the immobility of the earth were systematically criticised. But Galileo, acting on the suggestion of his faithful friend Mario Guiducci, did not neglect to warn the reader that his analysis was to be seen solely in the context of scientific, mathematical, geometric and astronomical reasoning, and that the Copernican thesis was assumed as a mere hypothesis, with the aim of explaining the apparent contradictions of the movement of the stars. The context of faith and religion thus remained outside such considerations, and the teaching of the Church was exempted from any form of arbitration which might be made on the basis of natural, philosophical or scientific reason.

Faith and religion belong to those "superior reasonings" which are guaranteed by the *magisterium* of the Church; they refer to an order of truth which cannot be attained simply by human reason. On the other hand, it was necessary to show the Protestants (Galileo and his friends, Faber, Scioppio, Cardinal Zollern and Campanella put much stress on this argument, in the perspective of an on-going cultural and religious confrontation with those who professed the Reformed faith) that the Catholic faith did not destroy intellectual commitment, indeed, it aimed to stimulate it to greater rigour, such as was required in order to know and evaluate the reasoning of those who had different convictions. Faith cannot be divorced from informed assent.[126]

Thus in Galileo's intentions and those of his friends who were most directly involved in the operation, Mario Guiducci and Ciampoli, the Letter was intended as a kind of sounding-out of opinions and positions, a first and limited and cautious taking up of positions as regards the Copernican thesis. Ciampoli was concerned with revising two or three points which could give rise to hostile interpretation, and he undertook to present the written text to the Pope, after first having stressed the opportunity to reduce the defence of Ingoli to its modest proportions, and hence discourage the intervention of amateurs who would end up, precisely because of their far from consistent reasonings and proofs, by putting the very decisions of the ecclesiastical authorities which they aimed to defend in a bad light. Urban VIII was therefore informed. Naturally in the most diplomatic way possible (as we have seen), of this new writing of Galileo, in which the Copernican text was re-assessed. Ciampoli, while minimising it, and stressing the fact that it was treated as a mere hypothesis, was obliged to point out to the Pope, in part because it referred to specific arguments put forward by Galileo to demonstrate the possibility of the movement of the earth: "I have read the reply to Ingoli, and I have also referred a great part to (His Holiness) who has great taste for the example of the value, and of those bodies judged little apt to movement, with those gracious experiments which you carried out".127

3. The 1616 condemnation and the re-examination of the Copernican question

But despite this early success, it was necessary to proceed with caution. There was certainly no lack of people hunting for a false step by which they could plunge the scientist into the consequences of the ecclesiastical censure of 1616. It was Mario Guiducci himself who exhorted his friend to prudence and a measure of reserve – convinced that the letter must have a wider circulation. He had had news that the Holy Office had given rise to a denunciation against the *Saggiatore* because the Copernican thesis was upheld in it; fortunately the consultant entrusted with the examination of the work, Giovanni di Guevara, the General of the Clerks Minor, had ruled out the attribution, but had also indicated the reasons why he did not hold that the teaching of the movement of the earth should be condemned. It was wiser for the moment, therefore, not to raise the Copernical question once again, also because for important diplomatic and political reasons, Cardinal Francesco Barberini was away, and because of the grave anxieties arising from the war, the Pope would not have been in a position to devote the necessary attention to requests for intervention aimed at stopping any further denunciations bringing about a new examination by the Congregation of the Holy Office.[128]

Meanwhile Tommaso Campanella had joined the group of the friends of Galileo in Rome intent on upholding the legitimacy of a more profound reconsideration of the Copernican question. He had finally been released from prison in Naples, and was in the company of learned men who expected a decisive boost to letters, the arts and to scientific and philosophical learning from the new Pope. He was also among the closest collaborators with the Papal court. Testimonies to the activity undertaken by Campanella in favour of Galileo between 1626 and 1630 are especially interesting if we seek to give detailed form to the role played by Urban VIII in fostering the conviction that it was legitimate to discuss and seek further knowledge on the Copernican question, above all as a comparison between the two systems, and that enquiries of this kind, conducted with the scientific rigour of which Galileo had given ample proof, would be seen with interest on the part of the church authorities.

The first of these testimonies is particularly significant, and although indirectly, because it was referred by Campanella to Cesi and by the latter to Fr Castelli, who wrote about it to his master, it is nonetheless very specific, because it records the actual words of the Pontiff. Certainly it may be that Campanella had reported the expression in such a way as to render explicit what was only implicit in the original, but even with this reservation it remains a fact that the Pope had given a clear indication of his attitude, of interest and even in some sense of openness – though within certain limits – to the Copernican question. " Father Campanella, speaking in these past days to the Holy Father, had told him that he had certain German gentlemen on his hands whom he was hoping to convert to the Catholic faith, and that they were quite well disposed; but that having heard about the ban on Copernicus, etc., they had been very scandalised and he had not been able to do anything else. And our Lord the Pope replied to him in these precise words: "*It was never our intention; and if it had depended on Us, that decree would not have been issued.* All this I learned from Prince Cesi…".[129]

The second piece of evidence is provided by certain passages in the *Comment* which Campanella wrote on the poems composed by Urban VIII during the time that he was a cardinal, in which the philosopher did not lose the opportunity to resume some essential themes of his speculation, above all those concerning the profound religious, philosophical and artistic renewal which would make it possible to rebuild that unity of faith and of the Christian community which had been destroyed by the Reformation. The pontificate of Urban VIII corresponded precisely with that programme; his poetry was thus considered as the manifestation of a very high inspiration, aimed at the genuine restoration of the faith and the truth, which could be brought about, as already mentioned, by a radical renewal. It is precisely in this perspective that we must consider the need for a new interpretation of nature, which must arise out of the new geographical discoveries begun by Colombus, and by the astronomical discoveries of Galileo.[130] And on the occasion of his comment on the ode *Adulatio perniciosa,* dedicated to Galileo, Campanella does not hesitate to call to mind the friendship which has bound him to the scientist since the days of Padua; how he intervened on his behalf in the process of 1616 with an *Apologia* which had been requested from him by Cardinal Caetani, and in which he showed that the theses sustained by Galileo were not in conflict with the teaching of the doctors of the Church; and finally he pointed out the very opportune interest of the Pope, then Cardinal Maffeo Barberini, that it should be permitted to study the Copernican system simply as a scientific hypothesis: "But our Divine Poet, raised to the Supreme Pontificate, (etc, Latin)".[131]

Campanello's comment must have irritated Urban VIII, who saw himself presented as a sympathiser of the Copernican system, even though Campanella had limited himself to recalling an episode known about by all those who had followed closely the question of the ecclesiastical censure of 1616. We are informed by the letter sent by the philosopher to the Pope in June 1628, in which after specifying that he did not personally accept the Copernican theory, he indicates the reasons why, with great wisdom, it was decided to avoid a somen condemnation of the Copernican system, which above all had been proposed by a scientist whose calculations had made possible the reform of the calendar carried out during the reign of Gregory XIII.[132]

4. The Dialogo dei massimi sistemi *and the ecclesiastical authorisation*

As soon as he had finished his reply to Ingoli, Galileo began to write his new work dedicated to the subject of "the flow and ebb of the tide", to him of key importance in the resolution of the Copernican issue. It was also supposed to be a systematic analysis of the arguments which favoured the heliocentric system. The work took him from 1625 to the early days of 1630, with alternating phases of "high and low", because of some periods of stasis: friends, above all those in Rome, more directly involved in the good outcome of his great new work, with Ciampoli in the lead, followed the composition of the *Dialogue* with the greatest interest, and almost with trepidation. "News has arrived here that the progress of your Dialogues is moving very slowly, and hearing this, we sigh for the loss of such rare treasures", wrote Ciampoli in July 1627.[133] And he exhorted his friend to bring this important work to a conclusion, not omitting to remind him of the benevolent and always lively attention which was being paid to it by the Pope himself.

The witness of Campanella, to which we have already referred, concerning the judgment of the Pope on the ecclesiastical censure of 1616, thus assumed a special value for the group of Roman supporters of Galileo, and naturally for the scientist himself, and it strengthened their conviction that they would be able to count on the personal involvement of Urban VIII to remove any obstacles which might be put in the way of publishing the *Dialogue*. In fact, Galileo had recently finished his work, and the question was really one of finding the most suitable way of resolving the last difficulties which arose naturally out of the decree of 1616, and how to obtain the *imprimatur* so that printing could go ahead. This initiative seemed to be eased by the fact that towards the end of 1629, the Dominican Nicolò Riccardi had been nominated Master of the Sacred Palace – in whose competence lay the permission to publish books – and he had already been approached in 1624 and had showed his favourable disposition towards the possibility of dealing with the problems caused by the Copernican system from a scientific standpoint. In fact in February 1630,

Castelli wrote to Galileo: "[…] I have many times spoken of you and of your great merit and quality to the Father Master, and even told him that you had resolved to write to him after His Reverence was appointed to the Office of Master of the Sacred Palace, because you were certain that it would not be as in the past, when things were judged by the ignorant. And his reverence replied to me that it was all in his hands, and that he would always have had the due esteem for your virtues, and that you should not doubt this. I certainly hold firmly that for his part, things are on the right track".[134] But if Fr Riccardi had been won over for the cause of the publication of the *Dialogue*, it was still necessary to remove some of the doubts remaining to Cardinal Francesco Barberini, who in his role as patron of the Academy of the Lincei, and because of the position he held in the papal court, was undoubtedly the most important figure after the Pope himself in the good outcome of Galileo's new initiative. In the same letter that we have already mentioned, Castelli informs his friend of a conversation and a subsequent private talk with Cardinal Barberini, in which some reservations were evident about the movement of the earth at the same time as a lively interest was shown in the work that the scientist was writing, so as to suggest a specific statement, in his judgment of great importance, as to whether the earth should be considered in the heliocentric hypothesis as a star – a statement which, however, must be considered contrary to a great deal of theological truth.[135]

But the question of the publication of the *Dialogue*, despite the highly authoritative protection which the author enjoyed, and a certain, albeit indirect, go-ahead that he had obtained from the Cardinal, was still a very delicate question, and for this reason his friends (Castelli and Ciampoli) thought it was more appropriate that the scientist should honour the Pope's interest with his own presence with the aim of removing the final difficulties. From Bologna Bonaventura Cavalieri wrote to him in February 1630 to express the conviction that the best moment had arrived to complete his work, and that he should not let the opportunity provided by the pontificate of Urban VIII slip from his grasp.[136]

In the first days of May, Galileo was in Rome, with the firm intention of making all the contacts which would finally enable him to publish his work, in which he and his friends placed so much faith that an objective, scientific re-examination of the Copernican question would be undertaken. But about ten days after his arrival, the Notices tell us that public opinion in Rome registered a first underhand attack on Galileo: he is trying to print a book in which he challenges many opinions which are held by the Jesuits, and as an astrologer he has predicted not only the death of Taddeo Barberini, but also that of the Pope himself, so that many are already talking about the election of the new Pope.[137] Even though this calumny provided an occasion for Cardinal Francesco Barberini to renew his declaration of esteem and friendship towards Galileo ("The Lord Cardinal said that Sig. Galileo had no greater friend than he, and the Pope himself, and that he knew who he was and knew that he did not have these things in his mind"),[138] it was nevertheless still a warning sign of the kind of reaction there would be on the occasion of the publication of the *Dialogo*.

A copy of the manuscript was consigned to Riccardi, who called on Fr R.Visconti to assist him in examining it. Visconti had special competence in the field of mathematics. Both Visconti and Riccardi – who had been informed about the work for some time – expressed their opinion in favour of printing it, though a few corrections should be made to it; indeed, Riccardi undertook to speak directly to the Pope about it "to take it away from the irritation which it causes

His Holiness that the demonstration that you wish to make that the flow and ebb proceeds from the movement of the earth",[139] as we are told by Orso d'Elci in a letter to Galileo dated 3rd June 1630. The Master of the Sacred Palace thus knew about the reservations of the Pope concerning some of the notions contained in the *Dialogo,* but he believed that he had singled out the points in which certain statements should be "attenuated" because they had aroused anxiety in the Pontiff. In this way the last difficulties would be removed in the way of submitting to the Pope the dedication of the work: "The Father Master kisses your hands and says that he is pleased with the work, and that tomorrow morning he will speak with the Pope about the dedication of the work, and that moreover, after adjusting a few small points, similar to those which we rectified together, he will give the book to the Pope".[140] It was Visconti himself who informed Galileo – a clear sign of the undertaking of the revisers in favour of the publication of the *Dialogo*, and of their conviction that such an undertaking would find a response in the interest with which the Pope followed the scientist's activities.

At the end of June, Galileo returned to Florence, after having been received by the Pope and by Cardinal Francesco Barberini, having finally obtained what he wanted, i.e. the go-ahead for the printing of his *Dialogo*. There was no formal provision, but he must certainly have received assurances on the matter from the Pope himself, who had already entrusted the mater to Riccardi. As Master of the Sacred Palace, the latter would grant the *Imprimatur*, and this was the understanding which the Grand Duke's Ambassador Francesco Niccolini, expressed in a letter to Andrea Cioli, the head of the Chancery of the Grand Duchy.[141] "Sig. Galileo left here on Wednesday last, with complete satisfaction, and with the entire fulfilment of his delicate negotiation, by merit of his courage and his very courteous manner. The Pope granted him willing audience, and paid him numerous compliments, as did Cardinal Barberino (sic) who again invited him to dine with him; and the whole Court accorded him the esteem and honour which is due to him".

This fourth brief stay in Rome, from May to June of 1630, motivated by the need to obtain permission for the printing of the *Dialogo,* poses a particularly important problem for the evaluation of subsequent events, which were to be characterised, as is well known, by a radical 'inversion' in the attitude of Urban VIII, concluding with the trial and condemnation of Galileo. We know that Urban VIII was troubled by "the demonstration that the flow and ebb proceed from the movement of the earth", but we must assume that Riccardi succeeded at least in attenuating that anxiety, because he certainly communicated to the Pope Galileo's wish to publish the work, and his own and his assistant's favourable opinion for the granting of the *imprimatur.*

Urban VIII clearly did not issue a ban on the printing of the *Dialogo,* which he considered could be published as long as the manuscript was revised in such a way that the logic of the exposition and the arguments of Galileo were in conformity with the provisions of the church censure of 1616, according to which the Copernican thesis could only be maintained as a mere hypothesis, and as long as the title of the work made no reference to the "flow and ebb" of the tide. He also recommended that the most careful consideration should be given to the argument which he had talked about at great length with Galileo himself in 1616, concerning the impossibility of demonstrating that the Copernican system was "necessarily" true. Urban VIII very probably did not read the whole of the *Dialogo*, but he was informed about it in sufficient detail by Cardinal Francesco Barberini. He therefore agreed, under certain conditions, that the printing could go ahead, in practice entrusting Riccardi with the task of supervising the fulfilment of those conditions.

Finally, it may be assumed that Riccardi, as an aspirant to the Cardinal's hat, would have taken great care to interpret the Pope's intentions accurately concerning the publication of the *Dialogo,* and to carry them out with every scruple.

The *Imprimatur* was only granted by Riccardi a year later, in July 1631. According to the agreements, the work was to be printed under the auspices of the Accademia dei Lincei in Rome, after a second check by the revisers of the corrections made by Galileo. But the death of Federico Cesi, the "Prince" of the Accademia, which took place in July 1630, caused the cancellation of the project of publication by the Lincei, while the spread of the plague in Tuscany made communications particularly difficult, preventing Galileo from coming back to Rome to provide for the printing of his work. In this situation, the scientist, the Ambassador Niccolini and his wife, who was Riccardi's sister, pressurised the latter to nominate a reviser of his own choice in Florence, and to permit the volume to be printed in that city. The Master of the Sacred Palace let more than a year pass before he decided: he was afraid that the revision did not correspond to the provisions that the Pope had made: "Fr Stefani will have given judicious attention to the book, but not being aware of the feelings of Our Lord the Pope, I cannot give approval as if it were only up to me to do so, in order that the book should be printed without any danger of containing something which displeased him and me [...] and this I cannot do with only the permission to print, which matter does not belong to me, but only with an assurance that it is in conformity with the rules which have been given by order of Our Lord the Pope, seeing that he has required them".[142] In the end he confined himself to asking Galileo for the famous Introduction to the *Dialogo* – in which, recalling the ecclesiastical censure of 1616, it is declared that "the Copernican section" should be treated "as a pure mathematical hypothesis" – and for the last pages, in which the discussion on the argument of Urban VIII had been inserted.

After having revised these two "parts", again at the request of Niccolini, who recognised moreover that "he has suffered quite substantial distaste and mortification as a result of certain works published a short time ago", and would suffer a great deal more a few months later – Riccardi finally sent it back to the Inquisitor of Florence, thus definitively confirming the permission to print with a letter which began with a very significant reference: "In conformity with the order of His Holiness concerning the book of Sig. Galilei [...]".[143] The printing of the *Dialogo* could thus at last begin, and it was completed by the end of February 1632. On the 21st of that month, the printer Landini told Marsili at Bologna that in the next days, the first copies would be presented to the Grand Duke, and provision wouold then be made for the sending of the volume to the other cities of Italy.[144]

5. *Supporters and adversaries of Galileo: the denunciation of the* Dialogo

The success of the work seemed to be a foregone conclusion: the eager expectation of both Italian and foreign scholars was a sure witness to this. The go-ahead of the church authorities, guaranteed by the *Imprimatur* of the Master of the Sacred Palace and of the Inquisitor of Florence, shielded the *Dialogo* from the attacks of ill-disposed and tenacious opponents. But in contrast, in the space of only a few months, there was a radical change in attitude towards Galileo's work, and this took place in the Roman Curia itself. It was to be followed by the decision to subject the scientist to a second trial. The documents on Galileo's case do not provide us with precise information about the persons who took the initiative to raise the question of the compatibility of the *Dialogo* with the doctrine which had been sanctioned in 1616, thus involving the prestige of Urban VIII himself. Certainly they must have been authoritative members of the Roman Collegio ("[…] and by the fine band, I mean the Jesuit Fathers have been in the lead above all, giving the impression that my book is execrable and more pernicious than the writings of Luther and Calvin", Galileo observed with bitterness in a letter to Diodati).[145] But other ecclesiastics too were involved, indeed, if we are to believe Buonamici, the "case" may have been provoked by the Commissary of the Holy Office, Vincenzo Maculano, in order to put the Master of the Sacred Palace, who had given the *Imprimatur*, in a bad light.[146]

We must, therefore, weigh up the information and indications which the correspondence offers us, taking account above all of the times and the modes of "penetration" (to use one of Galileo's own terms) of the first copies of the *Dialogo* in the Roman ecclesiastical environment. It should be remembered that the sending of the copies to Rome had been seriously held up by the provisions which subjected any commerce with the regions where the plague had spread, including Tuscany, to a series of rigorous controls and prohibitions. On 28th March Niccolini warned Galileo of the difficulties relating to the despatch of the volumes: "I would advise Sig. Galileo to postpone the sending of his printed books to the Lord Cardinal Barberini, and to the others, until the month of May […], because at present the said books will not be allowed out of quarantine, and without first being perfumed, and the covers and strings and all that may be suspected of contagion smoothed and scorched […]".[147] But Galileo had already sent a certain number of copies to Rome via Mons. Pietro Niccolini, from what Cioli tells us. We also know that

Riccardi, from what he tells the Inquisitor of Florence, had received a copy of the *Dialogo* at the beginning of March.[148]

The book had begun to circulate, even though only a few copies were available, in the Roman church circles in March or April, for Campanella, in a letter of 1st May, complains to Galileo at not having been included in the number of the "privileged" to whom the work had been sent: "Truly illustrious Sig. Galileo, who illuminates our century in no vulgar manner, I am most grieved that I alone receive your favours thus meanly [...] And now they are printed, and I know of this from French philosophers who have written me: and Your Excellency has not deigned to inform me nor to send me a copy".[149] Galileo, for his part, had warned his friend Castelli that the delay was due to the difficulty of despatching "a large part" of the books, "bound and gilded", in order to make a worthy present for his authoritative admirers and friends in Rome: he specified: "I understand that some loose (copies) have penetrated [...]".[150] In the end, Cardinal Barberini too, as Castelli tells us, had received a bound and gilded copy of the *Dialogo* around the middle of May.

Now it is hardly credible that in this period, i.e. between the middle of March and the middle of May, when various copies of the work were already circulating in Court circles and exciting discussion and comment, that the *Dialogo* had not been presented to the Pope either by Riccardi – who, it will be remembered, had the responsibility for overseeing its publication – or by Cardinal Francesco Barberini who certainly had no interest in hiding the publication. We must also suppose that on these occasions Urban VIII had laid stress on the arguments which were of great importance to him, in order to know whether his dispositions had been observed by the scientist. It is extremely unlikely that the introduction had not been shown to him, and that they had not pointed out to him the inclusion in the work of his own argument, of which he had spoken to Galileo in 1616. It is true that the correspondence does not offer us any indication from which we might assume that there had been some negative reaction by Urban in the period we have mentioned; in the months of April May and June, Galileo's correspondence, as far as ecclesiastical circles in Rome is concerned, registers the praise of friends and admirers of the scientist, without any note of reservations or remonstrances on the part of the church authorities.

On 29th May Castelli shared with Galileo all his enthusiasm for the new major work: "I will continue for the little life that is left to me, to study this book alone and from this alone I hope to find that relief and consolation which can be derived from the contemplation of the wonders of God in the heavens and the earth"; in the same letter he had been bold to note that the character of Simplicius was the perfect characterisation of the empty presumption of the adversaries of the Copernican system. "In fact I would like to say that I had to hold back my laughter when I met up with Master Simplicius, who seems to me so precisely to describe the Copernican system, in his simplicity admiring the idiocy of his whole school of thought".151 The character of Simplicius had also been noted by another of Galileo's friends, who had been carrying on his anti-Aristotelian campaign for some time; Campanella: "Everyone plays his part wonderfully; and Simplicius seems to be the plaything of this philosophical comedy, which at one and the same time shows up the foolishness of his sect, the empty words, the instability and obstinacy, and whatever else you like to mention".152

But alongside these trusted friends there were also people in Rome – and in other cities such as Florence and Bologna – whose faced "changed colour" when they heard the most recent work of Galileo being praised so highly, or who reckoned that Catholic Truth was one sole thing, and that is that the earth was immobile at the centre of the universe. Among Galileo's adversaries the proposal began to mature for recalling the attention of the Church authorities to the notions put forward in the *Dialogo,* and to the violation of the Decree of 1616, which could not be ignored without grave damage to the prestige of those same authorities. Some evidence from the Galileo correspondence seems to point to Fr Scheiner, who, as we know, claimed the discovery of sunspots in competition with Galileo, as the person who took the initiative to question the compatibility of the *Dialogo* with the principles laid down in the Decree of 1616. We know that for the period which we have been considering – April, May and June – Scheiner had not had the chance to recall the *Dialogo*; Castelli tells us this in a letter to Galileo dated 19th June: he had learned from the Roman bookseller that on hearing the *Dialogo* praised as one of the major works of the century "was moved with a change of colour in the face, and with a great trembling in the waist and the hands [...] and he told me moreover that the same Fr Scheiner had said that he would have paid ten gold scudi for one of those books in order to respond absolutely at once". We have no other information regarding Scheiner's response, but we may suppose that in the weeks following, i.e. towards the end of June or beginning of July, he had succeeded in getting hold of a copy of the *Dialogo*: his "absolutely immediate"[153] response was to have its effect in a different context.

It should be remembered that towards the end of June, as the letters of Castelli and Campanella that we have mentioned tell us, the character of Simplicius featured in the learned and malicious conversations of Roman Court circles as the prototype of the presumptuous clown, perhaps with more or less concealed references to the role which Urban VIII had had in the matter. Certainly there must have been many who smiled or even laughed at Simplicius and in the end, these utterances and "snide remarks" must have been seen as pointing to the Pope. It is certain that towards the middle of July Urban decided to subject Galileo's new work to a rigorous examination: on 21st July, Riccardi wrote to the Inquisitor of Florence for the purpose of blocking the further distribution of the *Dialogo* and requisitioning the copies still on sale. He was careful to warn that "in the book there are many things which displease, and the fathers want these to be adapted under all circumstances".154 Thus the investigatory phase of the new process began, and this was to be 'formalised' in the month of September, and then brought to a conclusion with a notification to Galileo that he was ordered to appear before the Court of the Inquisition in Rome during the first days of October. The episode provoked reservation, doubt and resistance, as in 1616, on the appropriateness of taking a decision which would in a certain sense be definitive on the Copernican issue. Two distinct pressure groups were formed, the friends and adversaries of Galileo, and they had their influence on the investigation and the trial. The trial was not, then a foregone conclusion, far from it. The resistance, the attempts to find a solution which did not enter into the merits of the matter, was to characterise the whole trial, as we shall see.

The first person to be involved in the Galileo affair, as we gather from the correspondence, was Filippo Magalotti, a relation of the Pope's family: one of the Magalotti womenfolk had married Taddeo Barberini, the eldest of the Pope's brothers. And it was in fact to Magalotti that Riccardi turned, immediately after writing to the Inquisitor of Florence, around 22nd July, to inform him of the negative reaction which Galileo's work had aroused in high places, and to call his attention to the fact that some reflection was being made on the book with the aim of correcting or suspending it, or perhaps even prohibiting it". He had also written about this at once to Guadagni to get him to inform the Florentine friends of the scientist. After about a fortnight, precisely on 7th August, Magalotti again wrote to Florence, this time to Mario Guiducci, to provide him with more details on what Riccardi had already told him, as he had had a chance meeting with him in San Giovanni dei Fiorentini in Rome. The Master of the Sacred Palace had insisted on having the two copies which had been sent to Florence: it was clear that there was an intention to stop the spread of the book and to take it out of circulation. The main preoccupation of the prelate seemed to be that in the coat of arms which appeared on the frontispiece, two dolphins of which one was biting the tail of the other, there might be a hostile allusion to the ecclesiastical authorities. He also lamented that the work had not been printed according to the agreements reached, in that the arguments which had been "interpolated" by the Pope were not included, and that "the work having come to the hands of His Holiness, and being found wanting in this, it must be rectified. This is the cover (continued Magalotti) but the substance must be that the Reverend Fathers of the Society of Jesus have taken it in hand gleefully that the work shall be prohibited, for this is what he said to me himself, in these words: The Jesuits will persecute him with great venom".155

The problem, then, seemed to have arisen from the fact that the text of the *Dialogo* appeared not to be in conformity with the dispositions which had been made in Rome: it was thus a matter of declaring a willingness to revise and correct those points which seemed not to be in conformity with the mindset of the church authorities. "If by chance something had been inadvertently left, especially concerning the above-mentioned, they will not cause you any problems, they would be ready to remove or change whatever is sufficient here to save appearances". The question, Magalotti said, should however be treated with great care and above all with reserve, explaining that in this way the conduct of those inside the Curia and indeed in the Congregation of the

Sacred Office prove favourable to Galileo: "I know that I do not need to remind you to proceed cautiously, not making me the author of what is indicated by me, for I am anxious to serve everyone, and Sig. Galileo above all, who so well deserves it, but Your Excellency knows very well under what obligations my house stands, and with what circumspection the resolutions of the reverent fathers must be spoken of in such important matters".[156]

Meanwhile, on the basis of information provided by Magalotti, since the first days of August, the Chancery of the Grand Duchy had begun to follow the progress of the Galileo issue, seeking to intermediate through Ambassador Niccolini, with the Master of the Sacred Palace, with Cardinal Francesco Barberini with the aim of requesting a calm and objective examination of the work. Rumours were in fact abroad of the calling of a special congregation, dedicated specifically to assessing the theses upheld in the *Dialogo*: "[…] I hear that a Congregation is to be formed of persons well-versed in this profession, before Cardinal Barberini, all of them less than well-disposed to Sig. Galileo", warned Niccolini in a letter of 15th August.[157] Six days later Campanella wrote in turn to the scientist: "To my great disgust I have heard that a Congregation of angry theologians is to be formed to prohibit your *Dialoghi (sic)*; and that it will have no members who know anything about mathematics or anything learned at all […]. I have doubts of the violence of people who know nothing of […]; you should, in my opinion, cause something to be written to the Grand Duke, that as they are putting Dominicans, Jesuits and Theatines and scholarly priests in this Congregation against your books, they should also admit Father Castelli and me […]".[158]

Initially, the question seemed to be assuming a precise political character, since it referred to the relations between the Holy See and the Grand Duchy, and to the sovereign rights and prerogatives of the latter with regard to a judgment concerning one of his subjects over a work which had been printed in Florence. Moreover the administration of the Grand Duchy had already refused to allow the question of Marino Alidosi, a Tuscan subject, to be judged by the Sacred Office in Rome. So it seemed appropriate in Florence to state officially the reasons why an inquisitorial procedure was not considered allowable with regard to Galileo's work, which had been published in full respect of the rules on ecclesiastical censure and after careful and mature consideration by the part of the appropriate bodies, both in Rome and in Florence. The *Dialogue*, it was stated, had been "presented by the author himself in Rome to the hands of the supreme authorities, and read and re-read attentively by them, and I will not say with the consent, but rather at the instance, of the author himself, all those elements which the superiors required were emended, changed, added to and removed, and moreover the same examination was made here, following the order and command of Rome". In the note sent by Cioli, the head of the Chancery of the Grand Duchy, to Ambassador Niccolini, the Pope himself was appealed to, though only implicitly, by the statement that the *Dialogo* had previously been presented, and that the publication had taken place with the prior consent of the Pope. A "guarantor" tactic had thus been chosen, which demanded respect for the procedures, set up by the Church authorities themselves, and the rights which derived from them. The letter in fact concluded with a radically innovative request of the inquisitorial procedure, that the heads of imputation against Galileo should be previously communicated to the Tuscan government: "However, His Highness, always inclined to support the good and to hate the malevolent, requests that the censures and objections which are made to the book, on the grounds of which its publication may be suspended or even prohibited, should be sent to him".[159] The note caused a certain embarrassment among the Church authorities; it raised the problem of who had given permission for the publication, whether it was Riccardi or Urban VIII himself, a question which was to be discussed during the course of the investigation and trial. When, a few days after receiving the letter, Niccolini communicated the observations of his government to Cardinal Francesco Barberini, calling the attention of the prelate to the fact that the work had been presented to the "supreme authority", the Cardinal remained silent for a moment, then, very diplomatically, replied that by "supreme authority" he must mean the Master of the Sacred Palace![160]

At the beginning of September, despite the rigorous secrecy imposed on the investigation, the first news of the Galileo affair began to filter through: Riccardi supplied it to Filippo Magalotti, who had shown himself to be a reliable and discreet channel, capable of reporting to the Florentine friends of the scientist, and one who could have been capable of urging certain influential people in the Papal court in the right direction. The Master of the Sacred Palace now found himself in a very particular position, because of the simple fact that it was on him that the responsibility fell for the revision of the work and the granting of the *Imprimatur*. He had therefore to defend himself and Galileo, and had every interest in seeing that the consequences of the initiative by the Holy Office were reduced to the minimum – in other words to a further revision of the *Dialogo* and the correction of those parts which were held to be distinctly in conflict with the 1616 decree. He had mentioned to Magalotti that substantially two points should be made in favour: the first referred to the lack of harmonisation between the intention mentioned in the introduction, to treat the Copernican system as a mere hypothesis, and the arguments later produced in the book supporting the heliocentric thesis. The second point was the lack of an adequate exposition of the thesis upheld by the

Pope concerning the impossibility of providing an absolutely valid demonstration of the Copernican hypothesis – a thesis which, above all, was attributed to an absurd character, namely Simplicius: "[…] and as for the arguments of Our Lord the Pope, which in truth was one only and can be found at the end of the book, but which had been put in the mouth of Simplicius, a character who throughout enjoys little esteem, and indeed is somewhat subject to derision and mockery".

Magalotti's impression, after speaking with Riccardi, was that the dispute, once the "incandescent" phase had passed, was "cooling", so that it was unwise to follow the line of determined resistance, but more appropriate to keep a watching brief on the initiative that was under way (Magalotti was referring to the Congregation which had been convoked to examine the *Dialogo*), always professing obedience to the ecclesiastical authorities: "Now it is opportune, if I may freely speak my opinion to you, to arm ourselves with patience, and since they are already busy with this Congregation […] we should let it run its course, and without pressure or violent action, allow for the negotiations to go on at length, because either they will meet up with insoluble difficulties in their deliberation (if they really wish, as they ought to do, to examine the matter) – and this will be assisted by the lack of intelligence in the majority of this profession - or they will tire themselves out, and thus the negotiations will die a natural death".[161] It was thus a matter of letting the question run out of steam in the difficulties of the investigative phase, profiting from the inevitable divergences which would arise as a result of the difficulty and complexity of the question.

It was to this point, in fact, that Magalotti called Galileo's attention, as he had previously expressed to his highly-placed Roman friend the concern that the work of the Congregation was the premise for getting the Copernican opinion "condemned and decreed heretical by the superiors": a formal declaration in this sense, on the part of the church authorities, was to be excluded, since as various churchmen who had taken part in the Congregation of the Holy Office had already declared, there existed a variety of issues regarding "divine worship", "controversies both in favour and against of some of which it appears that the Scriptures or the Holy Fathers most clearly […] and in any case all say that without any urgent necessity or without the declaration by means of a General Council neither one side nor the other will ever be brought to a conclusion". It seemed, therefore, that there existed a similar mindset as far as the Copernican question was concerned, since the geocentric hypothesis could not be assumed as a principle of faith with the consequence that the Copernican thesis should be considered heretical: this was why Magalotti was convinced that everything would be reduced to a "most pleasing moderation of your Dialogo, with the addition or removal of something where it would seem that there is the obligation to maintain the decree already passed in all its rigour".[162]

6. Urban VIII and the investigatory examination of the Dialogo

But the utterance of Urban VIII on the very day after Magalotti's letter to Galileo was sent, on 5th September, was of a very different kind. Urban was speaking to Niccolini, who had been received in audience to deal with questions concerning the relations between the Holy See and the Grand Duchy. The letter in which Niccolini reported to Cioli the outcome of this talk is of the greatest importance for understanding the hostile attitude which the Pope had developed in those two months (July and August) towards Galileo. When Urban VIII considered that he had been affronted in his dignity and his prestige, he did not hide his anger, and he made his contempt clear to his interlocutor. The ambassador recounts: "While he was speaking about those annoying matters of the Holy Office, His Holiness burst into a great rage, and suddenly said to me that our Galileo too had dared to venture where he should not have set foot, and in the gravest and most dangerous matters which could be raised at this time. I replied that Sig. Galileo had not printed (his book) without the approval of the Pope's own ministers, and that I myself had obtained and sent at my own cost the introductions for this purpose. He replied to me, with the same degree of wrath, that he and Ciampoli had twisted matters, and that Ciampoli in particular had dared to say to him that Sig. Galileo wished to do everything that His Holiness commanded, and that all was well, and that this was what he had known, without ever seeing and reading the book. He lamented the behaviour of Ciampoli and the Master of the Sacred Palace, even though it was said of the latter that he had himself been swindled, by obtaining his subscription to the book by fine words, and then moreover handing it over to be printed in Florence, without observing the form given to the Inquisition and by adding the name of the same Master of the Palace, who has nothing to do with printing outside [the Papal realm]."

In the course of the interview, Urban VIII did not fail to stress more than once the dangerous nature of Galileo's doctrine, admonishing the Grand Duke himself to intervene in order to avoid spreading such a "rash" opinion, which would have brought "great prejudice to religion and that of the worst kind that had ever been invented", and not to adopt an attitude of resistance "as he had done in the other negotiation because he would not emerge from it with honour". He then made it clear that he had already appointed a Congregation for a detailed examination of the *Dialogo,* once again exhorting the Grand Duke not to involve himself in this issue: "[…] and that he had decreed a Congregation of theologians and of other persons in various sciences, grave persons of sound mind, who are weighing word by word every detail, because it is a question of the most perverse matter which one could ever have in hand; he went back to lamenting that he had been deceived by (Galileo) and Ciampoli".[163]

Urban VII had thus adopted a position towards Galileo that admitted no further discussion. The ambassadors, and those who had familiarity with the Pope, knew very well that in these cases he did not appreciate being contradicted. Niccolini was convinced that there was nothing else to do at that moment than follow the advice of Magalotti: to abandon the "guaranteeing" line of resistance with the aim of asserting the rights of the Grand Duchy and attempting instead to resolve the question giving as much time as possible. "As far as I am concerned, if I were to give Your Highness my view, I believe that it is necessary to undertake this negotiation without violence, and deal with it rather with the ministers and Cardinal Barberini rather than with the Pope himself, because as His Holiness points out the matter is a rapid one, most of all when there is a desire to contest or to threaten or be bold, because then it turns hard and brings respect to no one. The truest (way) is to gain it with time and by turning adroitly several times and without too much fuss, also by way of the ministries, according to the quality of the negotiations […]".[164] This behaviour on the part of the Tuscan government, which had aroused "such a change"[165] in the Grand Duke, aimed at redimensioning the Galileo question in the eyes of the Pope a little at a time, was also suggested by the Master of the Sacred Palace, who counted on being able to see the work of Galileo again, and once the work had been completed, on submitting it to the Pope's approval and at the same time he advised against asking for any intervention in the

Congregation by Campanella and Castelli in defence of the scientist. The former, in fact, had had to answer to the Sacred Office for some of his works, while the latter was notoriously too close a friend of Galileo's.[166]

Meanwhile, the Congregation had brought its work to a conclusion and had decided to re-submit the *Dialogo* to the examination of the Sacred Office, for the latest provisions concerning the printing of the work; he was informed, some days after 18th September, by one of the Secretaries of the Pope, Niccolini, who had thought it advisable to return to Urban VIII to plead the scientist's cause once again. The Pope proved to be less indignant towards Galileo, he stressed that the procedure followed, that of asking for a special Congregation, outside the Sacred Office, to examine the *Dialogo* showed the scrupulousness used in considering the situation of the Grand Duke's mathematician. It was thus an act of respect towards the latter. But he re-emphasised his conviction about the dangerousness of Galileo's teaching: "[…] and that once more Sig. Galileo was his friend, but that these opinions were condemned about 16 years ago, and that he had entered into a real thorn-patch, which he could well do without, because they are annoying and dangerous matters and because his work is in fact pernicious and the matter is far graver than His Highness (The Duke) is persuaded it is […]".[167] In effect, Urban VIII had firmly decided to bring the question, which had arisen on the publication of the *Dialogo* under the examination of the Roman Inquisition: in the meeting of the Congregation of the Holy Office held on 29th September in the Quirinal Palace, the Pope: "Relata serie totius facti circa impressionem libri a Galileo de Galileis Florentiae factam, nec non praecepto eidem ab hoc S. Officio anno 1616 facto", ruled that the Florentine Inquisitor, in the name of the Congregation, should communicate to Galileo a regular order to appear before the Tribunal of the Roman Inquisition, in the coming month of October.[168]

The minutes of the meetings of the Congregations of the Holy Office, the Decreta, do not refer to the discussions which arose or to the opinions expressed in the course of them by the members of the College: they are limited to essential notes on the examinatory provisions which were made, or on the decisions. But according to a letter from Campanella to Galileo, written two days after the meeting of the Congregation on 25th September 1633, the decisions must have been preceded by a lively discussion, on the appropriateness of initiating an inquisitorial proceedings on the work recently published by Galileo. It was the last generous attempt by Campanella (he ran the risk of paying a personal price) to help his fellow scientist, and prevent the ecclesiastical authority from embroiling its prestige in such a complex and controversial decision: "I have done everything possible to be useful to you; and if I should write to you the very urgent and well-motivated reasons why one should not act contrary to them, you would be amazed. *Ex arcanis eorum sacris et politicis*. I was not admitted, and even so I informed an Eminentissimo, who held back the impetus of those against you, and dilated from Matins to Vespers; and yet I do not know if it has been done. But I do not hold out great hope, since I was not admitted and certain persons threatened me".[169]

The witness of Campanella is especially interesting: within the environment of the Congregation of the Holy Office, then, there existed a current which was against the initiative of a trial: evidently the "Eminentissimo" knew he was not alone, but was interpreting the opinion of other Churchmen who had taken an interest in the question. The statement of Campanella is confirmed, it seems, by a reference by Canon Niccolò Gherardini, who entered into relations with Galileo on the occasion of the trial, and tells us, in fact, that within the Congregation, a very high prelate sought to free the scientist from condemnation: "[…] my work was offered in his aid, which truly could not consist in other than warn him of some particular warning to his government. I was inspired to do this by that same Prelate, as the one who not only because of the effective recommendations which were made to him by those who were protecting the cause and person of Sig Galileo, but also in order to counterweigh in part the malign intention of another personage who enjoyed great authority in the Tribunal, was inclined to aid him escape from the imminent and over-severe mortification".[170] There are no indications to tell us that the "Eminentissimo" and the "Prelate" are one and the same person: but it is certainly the case that in the ambit of the same Court, to which Gherardini refers, there was someone who upheld the conviction that Galileo was right: most probably one of the Cardinals to whom the Grand Duke had written at the beginning of the process to commend to them the fate of Galileo – possibly Laudivio Zacchia, who did not sign the sentence.

As we have seen, the judgments expressed by Urban VIII on Galileo in the course of conversations with Niccolini, and the decision to submit him to the judgment of the Inquisition are in radical contrast with what he had said and done from 1611 to August 1630, the month in which he had granted the scientist an ecclesiastical pension of 100 florins. His esteem, praise and friendship, and his benevolence, were all of a sudden substituted by the most decided hostility. This change was brought about by two causes, which in a certain way sustain each other. One was of a personal character and the other of a political one. Considering that the argument to which such importance was attached was given to Simplicius, the ingenuous booby, an object of amusement and facile irony, and to hold that Simplicius was meant to refer to the Pope, was one and the same thing for Urban VIII, and so much greater must have been his indignation when Simplicius seemed to hold up for mockery his culture and his character as a humanist, a lover of the arts and sciences, an image to which he was very attached. And certainly Galileo cannot have taken any account of the doubt that he would have aroused by attributing the Pope's argument to Simplicius: if he had had it brought forward by the Moderator, Sagredo, then very probably it would not have provided a weapon which was extremely effective in the hands of his enemies, and he would have kept the esteem and benevolence of Urban VIII: in fact the scientist had not understood the real significance of that observation, and considered it completely marginal and substantially irrelevant.[171]

The second motive, certainly more important than the first, was of a political character. It was related to the very vivacious discussions which had arisen in the College of Cardinals concerning the policy which Urban VIII had been following towards Spain and the Empire, in a very delicate moment for the situation of the Catholic forces in Germany. On the occasion of the secret Consistory held on 8th March 1632, Cardinal Borgia had read a report in which the policy of the Pope was fiercely attacked, as in the judgment of Spain he had not supported the action of the Catholic Monarch to assist the imperial forces in their struggle against the Protestants. The discussion – which was in fact a real clash of wills – took on very heated tones because Borgia let it be understood that the will and capacity of the Pope to defend the unity of the Catholic faith was being called in question, and that thus the intervention by Spain and consequently by the Empire[172] for the calling of a General Council which would judge the Pope's achievement was legitimate.

This episode profoundly disturbed Urban VIII. Not only was his policy directed at maintaining the independence and autonomy of the Church – and hence aimed at containing the power and the influence of Spain and the Empire, i.e. the

Habsburgs, while he was being accused of harming the interests of the powers who were fighting for the defence of Catholicism, but an attempt was being made to present his policy as the consequence of a certain sympathy towards dialogue with the Protestants which would inevitably have favoured opinions and cultural and religious tendencies contrary to the 'authentic' Catholic faith. And certainly the possibility that an eventual Spanish intervention in the policy of the Church might also be legitimised at the religious level must have impressed Urban profoundly. He had realised the grave danger for the Church of an initiative of this kind in such a delicate political moment. The Pope acted very decisively to block the Borgia initiative, and the Cardinal himself was ordered to return to Spain; the Italian cardinals who had supported his move were forced to retract in writing, and return to their sees; but the danger that Spain would intervene in the internal questions of the Church was not entirely eliminated, since it arose out of the positive or negative result of the war in Germany.[173] Among the figures in the Curia involved in the measures taken against the "Spanish party" was, in fact, Giovanni Ciampoli, guilty according to the Pope of having helped Cardinal Ubaldini in drawing up the report, and of not having informed him that it would be read in the Secret Consistory. He was transferred from the Secretariat for the Briefs to Montalto di Castro [far north of Rome on the edges of the marshlands] with the order never to appear in Rome again.[174]

In this particular state of mind, characterised by fierce and constant anxiety over an intervention by Spain and Austria in the internal questions of the Church, Urban VIII was ready to accept the criticisms of the *Dialogo* by Galileo's adversaries: he perceived that the approval of the work, precisely because it seemed to be in conflict with the Decree of 1616, could have been interpreted as a clear sign of that benevolent concession to the "innovators" which would tarnish the principles of the Catholic faith – a formidable weapon in the hands of the Spanish party. He could not ignore the fact that representatives of an undeniably powerful and authoritative order like the Society of Jesus maintained that the book "is execrable and more pernicious for the Holy Church than the writings of Luther and Calvin". It should be added that the whole question of the *Dialogo*, from the beginning to the end so to speak, had been presented to him and fostered by Ciampoli, in whom he could no longer pose any confidence. If the Secretary of the Briefs had "betrayed" him in such a serious question, it could be maintained that in the matter of the permit to print the *Dialogo* he should also have suspected his good faith. And so Urban VIII, in some ways negating his reputation as an intelligent and prudent politician, always informed about matters in hand, did not hesitate to declare to Ambassador Niccolini that he had been "twisted" – with the evident aim of abnegating all responsibility for the publication of Galileo's work.[175]

The Church authorities, then, had been 'twisted'; their good faith had been betrayed; they had granted a printing permit to a work which, once published, had proved to be completely different from what it had been portrayed as by the author. They could not be in any way held co-responsible for Galileo's and Ciampoli's initiative, and they had not given even minimal support to the theories upheld in the *Dialogo* in defence of the Copernican notions, already condemned in 1616. But this justification, if it can be accepted – and only up to a certain point, as we shall see – as far as Urban VIII was concerned, really seems to have small credibility as far as the three ecclesiastical revisors are concerned: the two Romans, Riccardi and Visconti, and the Florentine, Stefani, who read the *Dialogo* and during a whole year had more than one opportunity to discuss the corrections and modifications and additions which should be made to it with Galileo. They knew very well, therefore, what this was all about, and they were perfectly well aware of the way in which Galileo had handled the complex and delicate questions, so that in certain cases they had requested the changing of this or that word, adjective or expression: they had therefore granted the permission after due consideration, because they were convinced that the Copernican thesis did not impinge on matters of faith, and also because the Master of the Sacred Palace – who, we must bear in mind, was aspiring to a cardinal's hat – was very sure that the Pope had given his consent to the publication of the *Dialogo*. Witness to this is provided by Riccardi himself, and indirectly by what Urban VIII said to Niccolini to explain his changed attitude towards the scientist. Riccardi had hesitated for a long time to grant the go-ahead for the printing in Florence, because the ecclesiastical reviser was not *au fait* with the direction in which the Pope's dispositions and opinions on the matter were heading.[176] The uncertainties of Riccardi over granting the permission to print derived from a series of "mishaps" which he had suffered as a result of publications which he had approved, which had then run into the rigour of the church censorship, so that, according to Niccolini, he had been "pulled by the hair" to allow the printing of the *Dialogo*. In the letter sent to the Florentine Inquisitor, Clemente Egidi, Riccardi specified the conditions to which the publication of Galileo's writing was subject, and called the attention of Egidi "that it is the wish of Our Lord (the Pope) that the title and the subject matter should not deal with the flow and ebb".[177] Urban VIII had been extensively informed about the scheme and content of Galileo's new work: he had expressed his decisively contrary wish to the title proposed by the scientist, *Of the flow and ebb of the tide*, because according to what Galileo had told him, this seemed like an express reference to the Copernican thesis.

And he had given instructions to the reviser that arguments favourable to the heliocentric theory should be presented within the context of pure hypothesis, and to demonstrate the lack of foundation of the experience and contrary arguments advanced by peripatetic philosophy, but without any reference to the Scriptures. Finally, he had requested that as confirmation of this general line, his own argument concerning the impossibility of coming to any objective knowledge of natural truth should be added to the work. On the other hand, as he admitted in the audience granted to Niccolini, he had spoken with Galileo himself about the questions aroused by a re-examination of the Copernican thesis: "[…] also, he (Galileo) knows very well in what the difficulties consist, if he wants to know, because we have discussed them with him and he has heard them all from Ourselves".[178] If we are to believe the testimony of Giovanfrancesco Buonamici, who drew up a report on the trial in July 1633, Riccardi, when he was challenged on the permission to publish the *Dialogo*, defended himself by maintaining that the approval for the printing of the work had been given by the Pope himself: "[…] who excused himself before saying that he had had orders to approve the book from His Holiness himself; but because the Pope denied this and became angry, the Father Master said that the Secretary Ciampoli had given the commission him on the orders of His Holiness. The Pope replied that no faith should be placed in these words: at the end the Father Master put forward a note from Ciampoli by which it was said that His Holiness (in whose presence Ciampoli swore that he had written it) commanded him to approve the said book".[179] In this way it is clear why Urban VIII considered that the Master of the Sacred Palace too had been "twisted"; despite the fact that he had fallen into such grave misfortune for which he was supposed to have been relieved of his duties, he nevertheless continued to exercise them.

7. The investigatory stage: discussions and uncertainties

After receiving the notice to appear at the beginning of October, Galileo, supported by the watchful interest of the Grand Duke and his Florentine and Roman friends, sought to obtain a long postponement of the summons, because of the serious condition of his health, and because of the difficulties of travel in a region where the plague was widespread. On 13th October he wrote a long letter to Cardinal Francesco Barberini, in which he declared that he was ready to illustrate with a lecture the reasons which had induced him to write the *Dialogo,* assuring him: "that I have not moved to implicate myself in this matter other than by zeal for the Holy Church, and to submit to its ministers those new findings which my long studies have brought to me", and specifying that among other things, he had decided on "this undertaking" because he was reassured by the "most holy precepts" of the Doctors of the Church, but also because he was confirmed in his proposal of "a very brief but most holy and admirable proposition that, almost as if from the Holy Spirit, issued without warning from the mouth of a person of great eminence in doctrine, and revered for his sanctity of life": a clear reference to the assent expressed by Urban VIII to the publication of his work. Thus he asked to be examined, and to uphold his defence before the Inquisition and the Church authorities in Florence; finally he confirmed his intention of obeying the orders of Rome.[180]

There was a new attempt on the part of Niccolini, after making contact with Cardinal Barberini and Cardinal Ginetti and another Cardinal of the Congregation of the Holy Office (whose name, however, he does not mention; probably the same 'eminentissimo' to whom Campanella had referred), to intervene directly with Urban VIII in the attempt to obtain a substantial postponement of the process. But once again the Pope was not to be moved in his determination, and repeated to the ambassador his conviction that Ciampoli and the Master of the Sacred Palace "had behaved badly, and that those servants who do not do things their master's way are the worst kind of household staff"; in particular, Ciampoli had kept from him the fact that Galileo's book was being printed.[181]

Meanwhile, on the part of the Roman friends of Galileo, an attempt was being made to support the scientist's position, by calling on the attention of the churchmen directly concerned in the matter: Castelli, apart from acting in support of Ambassador Niccolini, had intervened with frankness and decision in the circle of the Roman Curia, "in order that they should not hasten into a deliberation against such a noble, useful and grand effort by your worship (Galileo), openly declaring that by not following the due customs of this excellent and sainted Tribunal, everything would be turned to the disadvntage of the reputation and reverence which should be owed to it". He had spoken of the matter with the Master of the Sacred Palace and with his collaborators, warning them against the doubts that would fatally arise out of a sentence of condemnation, since it was very difficult in this case to specify the limits and indicate and assess the effects. In fact, Castelli observed – not without a certain touch of irony – "while it was indeed their task to prohibit the pages written by the hand of man, their authority did not, however, extend to decreeing that the earth should stand still or move; nor could they forbid God and nature to reveal to us in time His recondite secrets in thousands and thousands of ways". He had also involved the Commissioner himself, Vincenzo Maculano, and had shown him how the considerations of St Augustine on the criteria for interpreting Scripture specified that "this question, whether the earth moves or no, had been well penetrated by sacred writers, but not decided or taught, since it had no effect on the salvation of souls". Again, it was known to all that Copernicus' *De revolutionibus* had been well received by Cardinal Schönberg, as by other bishops and Pope Paul III himself, to whom it had been dedicated; and that it was indeed on the astronomical calculations of Copernicus that it had been possible to bring the reform of the calendar to a conclusion "in such a way that the work of N. Copernicus had been, it may be said, approved by the authority of Holy Church".

On the basis of all these considerations, Castelli did not hesitate to declare to the Commissioner of the Inquisition, who was preparing to examine and condemn the work of Galileo, "that he had no scruple whatever to hold to, persuaded as he was by the most effective reasons, and by so very many proofs of experience and observations, that the earth does in fact move according to the movements ascribed to it by Copernicus. And I have had dealings with the most pious and learned theologians on this matter, who have not put any scruple in my way. And yet, since all these things are as they are, I do not see any reason at all why Your Worship's Dialogues should be prohibited". We have no reason to doubt the witness of Fr Castelli, nor of the initiative he took to get himself included among the consultants of the issue under examination by the Congregation, so that the reasons which militated in favour of Copernicus and in particular of Galileo should be kept in mind, for it was clear that this was a matter of a decidedly controversial issue. There were reasons for and against the condemnation; there was no consistent opinion among theologians, among whom there were definitely those who held that the famous statement of the movement of the earth did not impinge in any way on the faith. We know that an opinion of this kind had already been expressed by Giovanni de Guevara, the theologian who acted as consultant to Cardinal Francesco Barberini, for whom no opposition existed between the heliocentric theory and the statements of the Scriptures. Moreover, it seems from what Fr Castelli states that the Commissioner himself, who was guiding the process, was convinced that in the matter in question, the authority of the Bible should in no way be involved. "The aforesaid Father replied to me that he was himself of the same opinion, that this matter should not end with the authority of Holy Scripture; and he even said to me that he wished to state this in writing and that he would show it to me".[182]

But the perplexities and debates concerning the question of Galileo – whether it was appropriate to take a decision to condemn, involving the authority of the Scriptures, were not confined simply to Curia circles and the collaborators of the Holy Office. They were to end up by involving the mathematicians and astronomers of the Collegio Romano, who according to the Galileo correspondence, must have supported the initiative for an inquisitorial process. In the middle of September, a very young scholar and former pupil of the Jesuits, Evangelista Torricelli, was keen to show his masters his full adhesion to the theses put forward in the *Dialogo*, and declared that he upheld Copernicus and was "of the profession of the Galileo sect"; he had spoken of this with Grienberger, and with Scheiner. Despite his appreciative comments, the judgments of the two mathematicians were substantially negative: the arguments put forward in the *Dialogo* were interesting, but no truly convincing proof had been provided for the heliocentric thesis, which could not be held to be true.[183] But this opinion was not shared even by all the students of the Collegio Romano: there were those who, instead, tried to call the attention of their colleagues to the validity of Galileo's theses. It was Fr Orazio Grassi, a personality in some respects of the front rank in the Galileo affair, because of the controversy over the comets, who had provoked dissension, animosity and resentment between the Pisan mathematician and the Jesuit mathematicians. Along with other colleagues, Grassi knew that the heliocentric theory was the one that best responded to the problems raised by the new astronomic investigations, and he had warned, actually during the course of the dispute, that the geocentric theory could not be considered as a principle of faith. It was necessary to leave aside all polemical spirit, and consider the question by ascribing the proper value to the arguments of a scientific nature: "[...] and since I was asked for my opinion last year on his book about the movement of the earth, I tried with all my strength to mitigate those spirits which had become so incensed with him, and make them aware of the effectiveness of the arguments put forward by him, so that some people were astonished that I, who had been judged to have been offended by Sig. Galileo, and thus would have little affection for him, should have spoken on his behalf with such solicitude".[184]

The discussions and reservations to be subjected to the judgment of the Galileo Inquisition finally had an impact on the investigations and on the whole course of the process. If we consider carefully the report requested by the Pope, on the whole matter of the publication of the *Dialogo*, and on the items of accusation which were brought against Galileo, on which the whole process hinged, we cannot help noticing that the extensor of the document, after having listed as many as eight serious imputations, suggested in his conclusion the expedient of amending the *Dialogo*, i.e to limit themselves to a series of corrections of the text which would bring out the hypothetical nature of the helio-centric theory, substantially in the same way as had been done for Copernicus' *De revolutionibus*, in other words, without giving any more ground to the accusations and the subsequent process: "[...] that Galileo has transgressed the orders, by leaving behind the hypothesis, and asserting in absolute terms the movement of the earth and the stability of the sun; that he has made a mess of the existing flow and ebb of the tide in the non-existent stability of the sun and movement of the earth, but these are the principal heads of accusation: moreover that he has fraudulently passed over in silence a precept imposed on him by the Holy Office in the year 1616, which is of the following nature: *Ut supradictam opinionem, quod sol sit centrum mundi et terra moveatur, omnino relinquat, nec eam de caetero, quovis modo, teneat, doceat aut defendat, verbo aut scriptis; alias contra ipsum procedetur in S. Officio. Cui praecepto acquievit et parere promisit [...].* All of which things could be amended, if there were to be judged to be some utility in the book, to which this grace should be accorded".[185] A somewhat surprising conclusion in some ways, because it practically deprives the accusations of any content, and reduces the whole question to a problem of revision of the text. And this reflects not only the opinion of the Master of the Sacred Palace, and his friends, but also that of the "High Eminence" appealed to by Campanella, and perhaps of Commissioner Maculano himelf, who had not hidden from Castelli his anxiety about how well-founded the main accusation was: it is, in fact, hard to maintain that the act of accusation was formulated without the favourable opinion of the Commissioner of the Holy Office.

8. The judicial process of 1633

All the attempts by Galileo and by Tuscan diplomatic intervention to obtain a lengthy adjournment of the time set for his appearance, in the hope that the process might be held in Florence, were in vain. It was to no avail that the scientist pleaded his precarious health as the real cause of his failure to come to Rome; in the Congregation held at the end of December 1632, Urban VIII ordered that Galileo, after a preliminary physical medical examination, if he were not gravely ill and thus prevented from moving, must be arrested and brought to Rome[186]. Galileo had no alternative but to obey; after leaving Florence on 20th January 1633, and halting for the quarantine period at Acquapendente, he arrived in Rome on 13th February, and was a guest of Niccolini in the Villa Medici. Even though there were several meetings of the special Congregation set up for the examination of the *Dialogo*, even though the investigatory phase was ended and the deed of accusation had been drawn up, Galileo was forced to wait a good two months before the judicial process actually began, and this despite the fact that his friends and the ambassador, on behalf of the Grand Duke, formally requested the ecclesiastical authorities for an examination of the matter. Evidently doubts continued to exist in the Congregation; reservation, perplexity, and not only on the appropriateness of deciding on a complex and controversial question in the context of natural science by using the authority of Scripture, but also on the reasons assumed for conducting the process in the first place.

In those two months, the Galileo issue continued to be under discussion. The scientist was able to get two authoritative members of the Congregation of the Holy Office to take an interest in his case: Cardinals Bentivoglio and Scaglia, and he also succeeded in getting the Grand Duke to write personally to these two, pointing out the particular interest which led to the question: "[…] to the Most Eminent Lords Cardinal Scaglia and Bentivoglio, who have shown that they understand it very well for me".[187] And possibly as a result of this involvement, Cardinal Scaglia had read and examined the *Dialogo* thoroughly and, making use of the clarifications and explanations of Castelli - who was still at this point the Papal mathematician - he understood very well what he would have to be judging. From what Guiducci reported to Galileo, the cardinal, after this careful reading, had changed his previous inclination - naturally, in favour of the scientist: "I am delighted again that that Most Eminent Lord, whom we will not name, has set out to read your *Dialoghi (sic)* with diligence, with the help of Father Abbot Don Benedetto, and that he has formed an idea of it if not completely contrary, at least very different and far removed from that which he had previously formed [...]".[188]

Meanwhile, it had been arranged that Galileo could continue to be the guest of Ambassador Niccolini at the Villa Medici while awaiting further decisions, instead of being held, as a prisoner, at the Holy Office. This was with a regard to his age, his condition of health and also to the consideration which the Pope aimed to show towards the Grand Duke. Profiting from this favourable readiness shown by Urban VIII, Niccolini once again tried to "represent" to the Pope the appropriateness of modifying the inquisitorial process, but he obtained nothing. In the course of his audience Urban VIII returned to his argument concerning the impossibility of formulating a necessarily true demonstration of the heliocentric theory; his evident irritation at Niccolini's observation which made reference to a consideration of Galileo is a further indication that in the circles of the Holy Office itself there was continuing discussion of the Galileo issue, and possibly there may have been some reservations on the impossibility of giving a scientific proof of the Copernican system.[189]

Galileo stayed in the ambassador's residence from the middle of February till the middle of April, for two months, waiting to be interrogated, even though Niccolini had appealed both to Cardinal Barberini and to the Pope himself that the process should move along as speedily as possible towards the "issuing of a judgment". But despite the discussions which had been held in the last months of 1632, there was clearly as yet no agreement on the line to be followed in the judgment, and opinions were still divided. On 19th February, Niccolini informed the Grand Duke's Secretary that in the last Congregation, Cardinal Barberini had intervened, to discuss the case. The only result had been that one of the Consultants of the Court had gone to Galileo "to hear what he had to say and how he speaks or defends his notions, so as to resolve afterwards as to what should be done or how to proceed with him".[190] Eight days later, on 27th February, referring to the outcome of his audience with the Pope, he noted that the case was still in the investigatory stage, and this meant that uncertainties and reservations persisted, which naturally had a bearing on the line that would be followed in the conduct of the judgment: "[…] and then I begged him to give an order that haste should be made, as he was so old and also in poor health, so that he could return to his native land as soon as possible. He replied to me that the matters of the Holy Office proceeded normally with some slowness, and that he truly did not know whether it could be hoped to deal with it thus speedily, because in any case they were still putting together the process which was not yet finished".[191]

Very probably, one of the most difficult knots to untie on the part of the members of the Congregation of the Sacred Office referred to the granting of permission to print on the part of the church authorities. The condemnation, though indirectly, would necessarily involve the Master of the Sacred Palace, and would have meant that he would suffer a "patent" of incapacity to fulfil his office of "supreme reviser". To prevent such a result, Riccardi had declared and continued to state that he had had the Pope's go-ahead. This information, despite the rigorous secrecy which was surrounding the investigation, must have been circulating in the environment of the Roman Curia, close to the Papal

Court and the most authoritative members of the Congregation. When there is discussion among twenty or so persons – ten members of the Tribunal and about the same number of their assistants and consultants, on a matter over which opinions are divided, it is virtually impossible to maintain secrecy, despite the severe penalties imposed by canon law on transgressors. On this point, apart from the witness of Buonamici already mentioned, we have a specific indication by Niccolini, who was particularly careful to send information about the process and what went on backstage: thus we learn that after the first interrogation of Galileo on 22nd April, discussion continued of the problems caused by the ecclesiastical approval of the *Dialogo*. "The matter of the book has not been discussed so far, and they are concentrating solely on finding out why Fr Master of the Sacred Palace should have given permission for it, while His Holiness says that he never knew anything about it, let alone giving the order for the licence to be granted".[192]

After two months had passed since his arrival in Rome, Galileo was called for 12th April 1633 to the Holy Office, and thanks to the interest of Cardinal Francesco Barberini, he was housed in the rooms reserved for the residence of the Commissioner of the Congregation. On 22nd April he underwent his first interrogation.

The line of defence followed by Galileo in the course of his first deposition was that he had observed the disposition contained in the decree of the Congregation of the Index; i.e. that he had followed the Copernican theory as a mere hypothesis. He had come to Rome in 1615 of his own will, to clarify and specify controversial aspects of his astronomic theories, and to make a contribution to the examination of the complex question, and finally to learn of the decisions made by the church authorities. Cardinal Bellarmine had, indeed, confirmed what he had written to

Foscarini: "The Lord Cardinal Bellarmine indicated to me that the said opinion of Copernicus could be held *ex suppositione,* as Copernicus himself had held it, and His Eminence knew that I held it *ex suppositione,* that is in the manner which Copernicus held it, as can be seen from a reply from that same Lord Cardinal expressed in a letter of Maestro Paolo Antonio Foscarino [...].[193]

From the minute taken at the interrogation, it does not appear that the Commissioner had confronted Galileo with the precept, showing him the formal deed, signed by the scientist, the witnesses and the notary. There would have been no need to make it the specific object of the interrogation in order to know whether Galileo remembered how the precept had been presented to him, who were the witnesses present, what formula was used; i.e. whether he had been enjoined not to hold or defend or deal with the theory *quovis modo.* Galileo could not have replied before a deed signed by himself: "I do not recall that anything else was said to me, nor can I be certain that I will remember what was then said to me, and even when it is read to me... I do not agree either that there was that particular *quovis modo,* but it may be that it was so, since I have no recollection of it, nor have I formed any other memory of it, since I had, a few months later, that confidence from my Lord Cardinal Bellarmine".[194] Evidently the Commissioner only had available to him the deed which is still preserved today in the record of the process, without the subscriptions required for the legal validity of the precept, while Galileo had shown the copy of the letter of Bellarmine, of which he possessed the original in Rome, and which confirmed his deposition.

Galileo could claim, therefore, in order to justify what he had done for the publication of the *Dialogo,* that the admonition/precept which had been notified to him by Bellarmine was perfectly identical to the ban imposed by the decree of the Congregation of the Index, known to all scholars, and for better reason than the church authorities predisposed towards censure: so the fact that the *Dialogo* was presented to the Master of the Sacred Palace in Rome and to the Inquisitor in Florence, that it was examined and licensed for printing, freed him from any imputation, especially that of having acted fraudulently, with the deliberate intention of knowingly deceiving the church authorities, and getting round the obstacle of the precept. He could have said more: he could have referred to the conversations held with the Pope concerning the publication of the *Dialogo*, but prudently, bearing in mind the advice of Ambassador Niccolini, he abstained from doing so. However, he did make an attempt to call Urban VIII into the case; in the record there is a declaration that the Commissioner and the Congregation, for obvious motives, allowed to drop: "[...] one morning Cardinal Bellarmine sent to call for me, and told me of a certain detail which I would like to speak to the ear of His Holiness before anyone else [...]".[195]

The Commissioner was careful not to insist. What did it refer to, this "detail"? Was it to the fact that Maffeo Barberini had intervened in favour of Galileo, maintaining that he should not be declared a heretic, nor was the Copernican thesis formally heretical, and this was the understanding which the majority of the Cardinals of the Inquisition had reached, and that referring to this precedent, the Pope had consented to the publication of the *Dialogo*? Galileo kept this detail to himself, nor did he speak of it in the subsequent depositions, nor was he requested to clarify it, to specify why he had had to speak about it privately to the Pope first, and why he could not refer it to the Commission and the members of the Congregation. In this case, the real intention of the accused was not sought; he was allowed to maintain his 'secret', very probably the reserve involved was in fact appreciated.

9. Galileo's "Confession"

The process of accusation had thus reached a dead end: in all the questions put to Galileo, there is insistent recourse to the precept, but the scientist in his replies offers no element of proof as far as the formal intimation of the precept is concerned, while he denies in fact that he ever violated it. It was this, after the interrogation of 22nd April, that proved to be the most dramatic moment of the whole trial; in the Congregation doubts had been expressed about whether the accusations against Galileo were founded, and about the way in which the investigation should be pursued. Valuable testimony to this is provided by the Father Commissioner himself, in a letter in his own hand, addressed to Francesco Barberini, dated 28th April, three days after the scientist was interrogated: "Yesterday, in accordance with the order of Our Lord (the Pope) I gave to their Eminences of the Sacred Congregation about the case of Galileo, the state of which I briefly described to them: and when their Eminences had approved what had been done so far, they considered, on the other hand, various difficulties about the way of pursuing the case and getting on with it swiftly [...].[196]

But the provisions made were obligatory: the case must go ahead, using all the investigatory means available to obtain the confession of his guilt on the part of the accused, in other words to get a declaration on the part of the scientist which would enable them to get past the stumbling-block represented by the precept devoid of the required essential formalities. In this way, it would be given *ex post* value on the basis of the confession itself. So it was a matter of subjecting Galileo to torture, and this – among all the various difficulties, undoubtedly seemed insurmountable to the Congregation, both because it was the practice in trials by the Inquisition not to use torture against elderly people (Galileo was seventy years old), and because such a provision would appear absurd and inhumane if applied to such an illustrious scientist, for whom a whole series of special favours had been shown, all, naturally, agreed to by the Pope himself, which had not been the case with any other accused person.

It is once again Maculano who gives us some information on this delicate and important question in the process: "[...] Galileo having strongly denied in his constitution what manifestly appeared in the book composed by him, from which there would be a need for greater rigour in the process of law, and less regard for the respect which had been shown in this mater".

In this way, the process risked becoming blocked. Galileo could not be absolved after the specific provisions made by the Pope; perhaps it would have been possible only to condemn the *Dialogo* and forbid its spread and reading, *donec corrigatur,* as had been done for the *De revolutionibus,* and as the ambassador had suggested. But a stern rejection of this course had been received from the Pope himself; there was no intention of using "greater force" with Galileo in the judicial process, as we have mentioned before. The Father Commissioner, therefore, suggested that it should be permitted to deal extra-judicially with Galileo, with the aim of rendering him responsible for his error and reducing it to the term, when he knew of it, to admit it. He must have noticed that the scientist, at the end of his interrogation, and committed to showing his defensive thesis, was too confident in his argumentative logic, and had run, without noticing it, into an "excess of defence", with a statement that was difficult to uphold: to the demand by the Commissioner that he should indicate the reasons why he had not communicated the precept which he had been enjoined to obey in 1616 to the Master of the Sacred Palace, Galileo had replied that he had not thought it appropriate to refer to it because the

Dialogo neither proposed nor defended the Copernican thesis but to reinforce his own thesis he had immediately added: "[…] indeed in the said book I show the contrary of that alleged opinion by Copernicus, and the reasons that Copernicus put forward for it are invalid and inconclusive".197 In effect it was a bit much, especially if said by Galileo. Certainly Maculano thought to recall to the scientist this statement of his which he could not deny; if this was his intention, then he must recognise that the arguments used in the *Dialogo* do not correspond to it, because they always conclude in favour of the Copernican thesis.

In the afternoon of that same day, Maculano faced Galileo with a dilemma, which later resulted in an outcome that went counter to him: either the declaration was true, and in that case it was necessary to recognise that the *Dialogo* did not correspond to it, or it was not true, and so it would be necessary to admit that he had written the work to uphold the truth of the Copernican theory. After a long discussion with the scientist, Vincenzo Maculano succeeded in what he aimed for, i.e. making Galileo recognise that he had "exceeded" in illustrating the theses in favour of the Copernican theory, or in other words to have insisted on presenting them as completely inconsistent with the reasons that went in favour of the geo-centric notion. He had not, in substance, put forward the Copernican theory as a mere hypothesis, but had ended up by presenting it as an "absolute truth": "[…] certainly he clearly knew that he had erred, and that his book had been guilty of excess, all of which he expressed with words of great sentiment, like someone who finds great consolation in the recognition of his error, and prepares himself to confess it judiciously […]".198

The confession of Galileo, and the admission that the *Dialogo*, as it had been edited, led the reader to recognise the soundness of the Copernican theories, were to provide the elements of proof to demonstrate that the scientist had in fact acted wrongly, knowing that he had violated the precept, and with the intention of deceiving the church authorities who had given permission for the printing of the book. The subsequent declaration that he had not held and did not hold the "condemned opinion of the mobility of the earth" was not enough to give validity to his defensive argument: the exposition of the Copernican and anti-Ptolemaic theories had gone beyond his real intentions. The clear contradiction of what he had stated in his previous interrogations, and of the whole argument which he had sustained in the *Dialogo* only served, in fact, to strengthen the argument that the Tribunal intended to prove: that he had acted with the intention of moving the obstacles represented by the precept and to safeguard himself by means of the permission to print issued by the church authorities, from whom, however, he had kept the precept hidden.

Very probably Galileo had not realised the consequences of his admission that he had "excedeed" and above all of the arguments that he had adduced to "give honesty", as the Father Commissioner remarked, to his confession: he was convinced – he had thought so since the beginning of the case – that such an admission would involve the mere correction of the *Dialogo* wherever there were expressions that might be seen as too favourable to Copernicus, as he had done for the *De revolutionibus* – and that after that the volume should be able to be freely distributed. It certainly seemed to him the less of two evils: on the other hand he had already recognised the disciplinary power of the church authorities in 1616 and had given his assent to the "salutary edict" of the Congregation of the Index. Nothing remained now but to renew it, even at the expense of a great deal of bitterness; he had hoped, along with his friends, that the moment had finally arrived with the pontificate of Maffeo Barberini, for a complete demonstration, from the scientific viewpoint, of the Copernican system, so that the premises could be laid down for a revision of the 1616 verdict. And this hope had met with a positive response, as we have seen, in the interest with which the Pope had followed his work.

During all these years, since he had written the famous letter to Madame Christine, he had always worked within the context of the Catholic Counter-reformation, with the same enthusiasm, the same zeal and the same conviction of those who intended to assert the primacy of Catholicism in the face of the protestant Reformation. And this did not mean a short-sighted defence of what was dead or what had become completely sclerotic, but an affirmation of the Catholic demand for truth, which is a profound commitment to spiritual and cultural renewal, that must penetrate, so to speak, philosophy and science. Galileo thus found Campanella at his side, even though their philosophical and scientific outlooks were distant and sometimes conflicting. The *Apologia* which Campanella wrote in defence of the scientist is in substance inspired by the common aim of recognising Catholicism as a constant point of reference of the new needs and new problems which had arisen as a result of the great geographical and scientific discoveries.[199]

The news of the intention of the Roman Inquisition to examine his work, the notification of the order to appear in Rome at the Tribunal of the Holy Office, the awareness that he must face up to a judgment, had affected Galileo profoundly; they had in effect taken away all confidence in him and in his capacity to convince them, and indeed in the possibility of being heard without any prejudice, and he was convinced of the uselessness of continuing to "struggle". As far as his conscience as a scientist was concerned, he would have to be content with the awareness of having reached the truth, and with this he would have to be satisfied, since it was very difficult, according to the ancient warning of Plato, to share it with the multitude, with those who understood nothing about it. He no longer believed in the "worldly" success of his work; basically, it no longer interested him that it should be crowned with official recognition by the ecclesiastical authorities – a recognition he had sought for so many years with such commitment. It was intrinsically valid before his own conscience as a scientist and as a Catholic, because he was deeply convinced that between science and the Word, as it is witnessed to us in Scripture, there is no contradiction. This is the real meaning of the thoughts that he had set down in a letter to Elia Diodati in the middle of January 1633, shortly before leaving for Rome.

So we can understand why his spirit was disposed to accept the exhortations of his friends to show himself to be amenable, to welcome the observations of the Court without contesting them, so as to put an end to this thorny issue as soon as possible. It was wisest to be meek and understanding to those who treated the cause with animosity, as if it were their own; a clear allusion by the Tuscan ambassador to Urban VIII: "I seem to have given a little encouragement to this good old man, by raising his spirits and by opining that he should press his case and in the parties which are forming. However, from time to time he goes back to finding this persecution against him to be very strange. I warned him always to show a will to obey and to submit to what he is ordered to do, because this is the best way of mitigating the heated anger of those who are bitter about it and treat it as if it were their own cause [...]".[200] Galileo only adopted this attitude with deep bitterness, and as Niccolini testifies, with real affliction: the evening before he went to the Palace of the Holy Office, in which he was to be detained for twenty days because of the investigations for the trial and the relative interrogations, Niccolini once again exhorted him not to get involved in a defence of his theses, either on the scientific plane or on that of Scripture, but to show himself to be acquiescent and thus close the question in the shortest possible time. "He claimed, nevertheless, that he could defend his opinions very well; but I exhorted him, with the aim of getting things over quickly, not to struggle to uphold them, and to submit to whatever they might desire him to believe or hold on that detail of the mobility of the earth. He is greatly afflicted by this, and for myself, I have seen what he has landed in as a result of this, and I have great doubts about the safety of his life".[201]

The ambassador's words snuffed out in Galileo the will to resist that had been reborn in him just as the process was about to begin. There was no option but to entrench himself behind Bellarmine's letter; to assume as a line of defence the fact that he had attempted to deal with the Copernican theory and that of Ptolemy in a purely "hypothetical" way, without entering in any way into the merits of the question. Basically he had to return to declaring what he had already professed in 1616, on the occasion of Bellarmine's warning; what he had publicly admitted both in his letter to the Archduke Leopold and in the *Saggiatore* and in the *Lettera all'Ingoli*, that the ultimate decision on the question belonged to a more sublime doctrine. On the other hand, what he felt particularly strongly was that no shadow of doubt whatever should be cast on his faith as a total adhesion to the Christian truth represented by the Church: of this, he was ready to give abundant testimony.

On 10th May 1633, Galileo was called once again to the Holy Office and a limit of eight days was imposed on him to present his defence. On that same day the scientist handed over to the Tribunal the original of Bellarmine's latter, issued to him in 1616, and a defensive memorandum in his own hand, aimed at showing the reasons which had induced him to request that letter, and the value which the document assumed in the whole matter of the printing of the *Dialogo*.[202] In substance he repeated his negative response to the fact that the precept was enjoined on him in the form of "tenere defendere vel quovis modo docere": the letter issued to him at his own request by Bellarmine, witnessed in fact that that same ban which was contained in the decree of the Sacred Congregation of the Index had been notified to him, and that he had appealed to all that certainly he felt obliged to respect it, without it becoming a particular obligation for him. Thus, like all those whose work might have run up against the ban of the Index, he had submitted the *Dialogo* to the revision of the "Supreme Inquisitor", i.e. the Master of the Sacred Palace, to whom, however, he had not made any mention of the intimation which had been made to him by Bellarmine – "the precept (was) imposed on me privately, being the same as that of the Congregation of the Index". So he, although using the term 'precept' wrongly – remember that he was not assisted in the whole course of the process by a lawyer – referred to the admonition, which in practice imposed the same ban as the decree of the Congregation of the Index. For the rest, Galileo recognised (once again) that he had 'exceeded' in the form as far as the defence of the Copernican thesis was concerned, certainly in some senses favouring it over the Ptolemaic theory, and he declared himself ready "to redeem and amend" this "lack" "with all possible industry, at any time that I am either commanded or permitted to do so by the Eminent Lords".203

The perplexities and reservations over concluding the trial with a condemnation in clear contradiction to the church's approval of the *Dialogo* are characteristic of the process from the first days of June, and must have been the real reason why they opposed a speedy resolution of the case, as requested repeatedly by Niccolini, and which, after Galileo's "confession" of 27th April, could have been defined otherwise in about three weeks. In the first days of May, Niccolini had the impression, according to what the Commissioner General himself, Vincenzo Maculano, had said to him, that in fact the intention was to "consign the case to the archives", and make peace all round, more or less the same solution as had been adopted in 1616: "Signor Galileo was sent to me yesterday at my house, when I didn't expect him, since his examination is not yet completed; and this occurred as a result of the good offices of the Father Commissioner to Cardinal Barberini who on his own initiative and without the Congregation, has caused him to be freed so that he may recover from his discomfort and his usual illnesses, which caused him to be constantly under strain. The Commissioner also expresses his intention of wanting to make provision that this case be terminated, and that silence be imposed, and if this is obtained it will cut short everything and free many people from trouble and danger".[204]

Again at the end of May, after Galileo's second disposition, Niccolini held that a "compromise" solution could be found, which would avoid the "prohibition" of the *Dialogo* allowing the author to draw up, as he himself had proposed, a kind of apologia and clarification of his real intentions, even though it now seemed inevitable that the scientist would suffer "some salutary penance, claiming that he had transgressed the orders of 1616 given to him by Cardinal Bellarmine [...]".[205] But once more, the decision – which according to the Pope's declaration should have been made in the Congregation of 30th May, was postponed. It was necessary to wait a further two weeks; only in the Congregation of 16th June, meeting in the Papal Palace of the Quirinale, with six cardinals out of ten present (Bentivoglio, Scaglia, Antonio Barberini (the Pope's brother), Gessi, Verospi and Ginetti), did Urban VIII, after hearing the opinions of the members of the Tribunal, decree that Galileo must be interrogated once again on his real intention, and condemned him also to torture if his replies were not truthful. And, after making a solemn abjuration before the Congregation, he was to be condemned to prison, with the injunction not to deal in any way whatsoever, either in writing or in the spoken word, with the question of the movement of the earth and the immobility of the sun. The *Dialogo* was to be prohibited, and a copy of the sentence was to be sent to Apostolic Nunzios and to all Inquisitors; in particular the Florentine official was to hold a public reading of the sentence to the largest number of mathematicians possible.[206] In the audience of 19th June, the Pope informed the Tuscan Ambassador of the decision that had been reached in the case, and assured him that he would seek, because of the esteem in which he held the Grand Duke, "to mitigate the effects of the condemnation", "but that as far as the case itself was concerned, it would not be possible to avoid banning that opinion, because it is erroneous and contrary to the Holy Scriptures, dictated *ex ore Dei*".[207]

Two days later, Galileo underwent the final interrogation "super sua intentione": he repeated what he had maintained during the course of the trial process, which corresponded moreover to what he had stated in the *Saggiatore* and in the introduction to the *Dialogo*: The Ptolemaic thesis, and the Copernican, were equally valid in the light of the reasons which could be adduced for one or the other; as far as the *Dialogo* was concerned, he had taken care to illustrate all the arguments which could be put forward for one thesis or the other "using my skills to make it clear that neither the former nor the latter, neither because of this opinion or that, had the strength to prove conclusively, and that thus in order to proceed with assurance, one must have recourse to the most sublime doctrine, as certainly in very many places in the said *Dialogo* it can be seen to be stated".[208] The question concerning his intentions was put twice, according to the formula *rigoroso esame*: *nisi se risolvat fateri veritatem, devenietur contra ipsum ad remedia iuris et facti opportune*, and again, with a clear indication of the appropriate remedies, *Et ei dicto, quod dicat veritatem, alias devenietur ad torturam*; Galileo confirmed the previous declaration he had made, with words which indicated that the decision made to show obedience had caused him to adopt an attitude of substantial detachment: "[…] moreover, I am here in their hands, let them do what they please […]. I am here to show my obedience".209

10. The sentence of condemnation: doubts and reservations.

The day after the last interrogation, Galileo appeared before the Congregation of the Holy Office, meeting in the Dominican convent of Santa Maria sopra Minerva, to hear the sentence and to make the solemn abjuration of the Copernican thesis. According to what Antonio Badelli tells us in the *Avvisi di Roma* of 25th June, "they burned his book which deals with the movement of the earth before his face […]".210 The sentence referred back to the earlier trial of 1616, the conclusions which had been reached as regards the two propositions of the immobility of the sun and the movement of the earth, and it stressed the fact that "wishing at that time to deal with you with benignity", it had limited itself to issuing a regular precept to him not to follow the Copernican opinion any further: "[…] a precept was issued to you, notarised and witnessed, by the Father Commissioner of the Holy Office, that you must altogether leave off that false opinion, and that in the future you might not hold nor defend nor teach it in any way, either in speech or in writing". The publication of the *Dialogo* was thus a clear violation of the decree of the Congregation of the Index and of the precept, undertaken with the specific intention of getting around the ban, both in the editing of the *Dialogo* in which the arguments in favour of the

Copernican thesis "put forward in such a guise that for their effectiveness they were powerful to be accepted rather than easy to undo", and in the request for ecclesiastical approval, obtained by tricks: "[…] nor does the licence absolve you, which you extorted by deceit and craft, not making note of the precept which you had (been given)". Thus Galileo's conduct was clearly shown to be ill-intentioned, and this constituted the necessary presupposition for the condemnation, and placed the church authorisation for the licence to print completely out of court. Finally the sentence sanctioned in solemn fashion, reinforcing the decree of 1616, the statement that the heliocentric thesis was "a false doctrine contrary to the Sacred and Divine Scriptures", so that Galileo, for having held it and believed it, had "rendered himself vehemently suspect of heresy": the Copernican teaching, therefore, was no longer "bold" but formally heretical.[211]

It should be noted above all that the decision of the Congregation of the Holy Office does not make any further reference to the preceding deliberation adopted, if we can put it this way, in the "Council Chamber" under the presidency of the Pope, who pronounced the enactment of the sentence. From the formal point of view, the latter emanated exclusively from the Congregation, which as a tribunal was constituted by ten cardinals "in the whole of the Christian Community specially deputed as Inquisitors General of the Holy Apostolic See against heretical wickedness". The sentence did not involve the authority of the Pope, especially with regard to the delicate question of whether the geocentric theory was a matter of faith, and thus irrevocable and unchangeable. The sentence seemed to resolve the uncertainties and perplexities which had characterised the whole process as we have seen, in the way desired by Urban VIII; in effect, a careful reading and comparison between the decree of the sentence, and the formula with which it was "closed", shows us that of the ten cardinals who made up the tribunal, only seven (Felice Centini, Desiderio Scaglia, Antonio Barberini, Berlinghiero Gessi, Fabrizio Verospi, Guido Bentivoglio and Marzio Ginetti) pronounced and subscribed the sentence; three (Gaspare Borgia, Francesco Barberini, the Pope's nephew, and Laudivio Zacchia) did not take part in the Congregation of 22nd June, and did not sign the sentence.[212] We have no documents or witnesses which could provide us with precise indications of a positive kind about the motives which caused the absence and the non-subscription of these three cardinals. In the present state of research, we cannot do other than register the fact and seek to assess it on the basis of the whole manner in which the process took place.

From the "Decrees" published by Favaro, it seems that in the meetings of the Congregation, almost always presided over by the Pope (Paul V and Urban VIII), the presence of the cardinals varied from six to seven; only once were nine present, at the meeting of 25th November 1615. Clearly in the practice of the Congregation no criterion had been fixed concerning the presence of these ecclesiastics, so that certain cardinals could be absent from several meetings of the Congregation in which the same case was under discussion, without this being an impediment to the pronunciation and subscription of the sentence, or so it seems. In nine meetings of the Congregation which discussed and passed judgment on the Galileo case between 23rd September 1632 and June 1633, Francesco Barberini took part only in those of 23rd September and 30th December 1632, while Laudivio Zacchia did not attend the last two meetings of 16th June and 22nd June 1633. There are very few references to the fact that the Congregation should have pronounced the sentence *al completo*; in the registration of the Congregation's deliberation of 16th June, it is said that

Galileo must make the solemn abjuration *in plena Congregatione S. Officii*;[213] in the audience of 19th June, Urban VIII told Niccolini that he did not know "yet what the Congregation was about to resolve, but that it was heading unitedly and *nemine discrepante* in the direction of imposing a penance".[214] Given the importance of the question, in which his own responsibility had been called in question, however indirectly, had Urban VIII requested, or at least expected, that the all members of the Congregation should be present on the occasion of the pronouncement and subsequent subscription of the sentence? We would imagine this to be the case: the presence of all the members of the Tribunal would have witnessed without any shadow of doubt to the unanimity of the judges' agreement. Urban VIII had referred to this in his discussion with Niccolini, and it was on such a unity that a sentence which defined an opinion contrary to the Scriptures as heretical had to be based. We have no information about impediments (such as illness) or absence from Rome of these three cardinals: they were on the spot, and did not take part in the Congregation's meeting of 22nd June. This absence gives rise to some doubt, which may be well-founded, that Borgia, Zacchia and Barberini did not intend to lend their presence and their signatures to the sentence of condemnation. In certain very important cases – and Galileo's case is certainly such – the absence of those who had the responsibility to pass judgment, and in this case to defend the unity of the Church against heresy, and who thus had the duty to express their judgment through the sentence, takes on the significance of a sign of dissent from the decision, or at least of reservation and perplexity.

Very probably their dissent was connected with the solemn form of the declaration: that the Copernican theory was false and erroneous in philosophy and contrary to the Scriptures, and also to the solemn abjuration on the part of

Galileo. They knew, as indeed the others did, that the Copernican theory turned on a question of fact, and thus could not be judged to be *absolutely false,* for the same reason that the then Cardinal Maffeo Barberini had observed to Galileo that it was not possible to prove it to be *absolutely true.* A question of fact could always be demonstrated by a series of conclusive proofs, which could be provided by astronomic studies and research which it was not intended to forbid or to limit: otherwise the premise would make no sense, i.e. that the Copernican theory was false and erroneous in philosophy, in other words according to human reasoning, according to the scientific knowledge that was founded on the study of nature. Thus it was not a question of faith, in which the authority of Scripture should be involved with such a cut and dried resolution. It was necessary to stick to the criteria followed in the 1616 process, in particular in the Decree of the Congregation of the Index: the *Dialogo,* like the *De revolutionibus,* would have to be corrected, not prohibited with a solemn formula, so as to create a radical opposition between the theories of the two scientists and the Scriptures. The heliocentric theory would still have remained 'bold', the traditional interpretation of Scripture would have been re-asserted, and the freedom of scientific enquiry in the context of the probable and the hypothetical would have been guaranteed. And then we may believe that to various cardinals, experts of the Curia, and canon lawyers, that precept, not subscribed by either a notary or by witnesses, nor – and this was even more important – by the person to whom its was destined, must have seemed a document of little juridical value to uphold the accusation against Galileo. So too the assertion that the scientist had tricked the Master of the Sacred Palace, his assistant and the Inquisitor of Florence, and that these people had taken on themselves the sole responsibility for the printing, without being sure of assent "in high places", must have aroused some doubts in those – and there were several in the Congregation – who knew the people involved in the affair, and could not hold that the scientist was so 'diabolical' and the others so unprepared and ingenuous, above all after the declarations by the Master of the Sacred Palace that explained quite clearly why he had granted the permission to print. Indeed it was somewhat exaggerated to claim that Galileo had acted 'with ill intent'.[215]

The absence of the signatures has been interpreted as the result of a compromise by which, at the end, the Congregation had overcome some reservations arising from the various difficulties to which Commissioner Maculano referred.[216] This theory assumes a consistently critical attitude in the body sitting in judgment concerning the line of conduct of the process and the consequent decision; possibly it was not expressed as such in the Congregation itself, as an act of respect to the Pope (it should not be forgotten that Riccardi "affirmed" and Urban VIII "denied") who was directly interested in the question. They limited themselves, in point of fact, to not attending the concluding meeting of the Congregation, and not signing the sentence.

11. The Galileo question and the heliocentric theory in the decrees of the Holy Office (1741-1820): the 'revision' of the condemnation

The sentence of 22nd June 1633 had condemned Galileo and declared the heliocentric notion to be "formally" heretical. In the intention of Urban VIII, this would re-establish the conformity and unity of the scientific and cultural lines of thought to the traditional theory. But the sentence, after its spread in Italian and foreign learned circles, was not show to slow its 'boomerang effect'; it bounced back on those who had promoted and justified it, bringing them face to face with the problem which Galileo had dramatically experienced on the occasion of his subscription to the abjuration. "When Froidmont or others have established that to say the earth moves is heresy, and the proofs, observations and necessary calculations show that in fact it does move, in what sort of a tricky position will the Church then have placed itself?".[217] Thus the sentence was a "tricky situation", not only because it seemed to have sanctioned a cosmological theory – and thus a question of fact - as a doctrine of the faith, but because it seemed to involve a very serious limit in the context of scientific research, which many promoters of the process were not willing to accept – beginning with Scheiner himself. Instead of fostering the harmony and unity of the philosophical and scientific trends, it had introduced division and reservation which would not be slow to make their effect felt, and which would end by revealing the true nature of the sentence, by implicitly repudiating its substantial limitations. Ascanio Piccolomini, Archbishop of Siena, began to voice criticism barely a month after the conclusion of the process, when he had the opportunity of receiving Galileo as a guest on his way back from Rome. The statement presented to the Holy Office tells us that the Archbishop "had suggested to many that he (Galileo) had been unjustly attacked by the Sacred Congregation, and that he neither could nor should reprove the philosophical opinions which he had upheld with invincible mathematical and true reasonings, and that he is the leading man in the world, and will live for ever in his writings, even though prohibited, and that he will be followed by all the best modern (thinkers)".[218] The statement, forwarded in February 1634, was examined, but had no follow-up; they limited themselves to including it in the file of the Galileo process. Evidently there must have been several in the Congregation who held that the Archbishop of Siena was not wholly wrong.

In 1635, the request by the Jesuit Inchofer (who had been a consultant in the process against Galileo) to publish a work of his in defence of the sentence of the Holy Office against "the new Pythagorean supporters of the movement of the earth and the immobility of the sun" was not accepted by the revisers of his own Order, who refused approval for its printing. Evidently again, there was no intention to give credence to the decision in formal terms by basing it on the assertion of the geocentric theory contained in the sentence – a complex question on which differing opinions existed even among the mathematicians of the Collegio Romano. By approving the publication, there maight have been a risk that the personal opinion of Inchofer should appear to be the official one of the Order. The Society of Jesus thus considered it to be more 'prudent' not to commit itself to an *apologia* for the sentence, and so *de facto* took its distance, with all due reservation, from the decision of the Holy Office.[219]

In the world of foreign scholars, above all in France and the Netherlands, cautious but specific distinctions and reservations began to appear a few years after the process, in the sense that the sentence had not stated a principle of faith; that the declaration of heresy as regards the movement of the earth was not absolute but relative, in other words, limited to the episode of the Galileo process. Froidmont himself, possibly foreseeing the "tricky situation", had declared even in the text that he wrote to combat the heliocentric system, that he "had would not have dared to accuse the Copernicans of heresy, had he not seen a far more specific decree issued by the Supreme Pastor of the Church".[220] In substance, despite the sentence of the Holy Office, the question concerning the planetary system was to be discussed in the context of natural philosophy or science, precisely because there was no specific and authentic doctrinal definition of the faith on this point. The observation of Froidmont was taken up and given further significance by very authoritative French philosophers and scientists, who had followed the case of Galileo with close interest: Descartes, Mersenne and Gassendi.[221]

The question concerning the sentence, posed as we have seen by the friends and even the adversaries of Galileo, was re-examined in a systematic way by the Jesuit astronomer Gian Battista Riccioli, in his *Almagestum Novum*, published in Bologna in 1651. This is a ponderous work, in which all the scientific arguments in favour of the geocentric theory are reviewed, and compared with those favourable to the Copernican system and those upheld by Galileo, to provide a complete justification for the sentence. But just such a careful and in-depth examination brought out the fact that there were no necessarily conclusive and thus absolute proofs in favour of the geocentric system, such as would exclude the Copernican theory. After observing that the principles of the faith must be defined as such either by the Pope or by a General Council presided over and approved by the latter, Riccioli was careful to specify that "it is no longer a matter of faith that the sun moves and the earth is still; but at the most it is only in virtue of the Holy Scriptures for those for whom it is morally certain that God has revealed it to be so. All we Catholics, however, in our duty of prudence and obedience, are held to hold to what the Congregation has laid down, or at least not to teach the contrary in absolute form".[222] This emphasised the very specifically disciplinary nature of the sentence, which referred to the particular event of the publication of the *Dialogo*, and to the way in which the Copernican theory had been put forward. But Riccioli's observations did not prevent Huygens from revealing, with a touch of malice, that the French (catholic) astronomers were teaching the Copernican theory not as a mere hypothesis but as a theory which corresponded with reality, without the Holy See taking any measures to condemn them. The Jesuit Fabri, challenged on the matter by the Dutch scientist, thus found himself forced to admit that the geocentric theory would certainly be abandoned if certain proof of the Copernican system were to be adopted.[223]

These points having been made, the 1633 sentence ought to have been interpreted as a mere provision of a disciplinary character: it did not refer so much to the Copernican teachings and those of Galileo, as to the form and the manner in which the scientist had upheld them. This was the way in which, as we have mentioned, the Jesuit mathematician Antonio Baldigiani put it in a letter to Viviani dated 18th July 1678: "[...] so now it is no longer Galileo that is condemned for his teachings, nor is it being said that it is heresy against Scripture, of dubious faith, but what is disputed is the way in which he wrote which is a very different question from the former".[224] Leibniz also expressed a similar viewpoint, when he stressed that the sentence of 1633 must be considered a completely provisional ruling, while waiting for the question raised by Galileo to be examined in the light of new discoveries in physics and mathematics.[225]

In these same years, when Newton was drawing up his theory of universal gravity, precisely in 1686, another Jesuit mathematician, Adam Kochansky, who had taught in the Florentine Collegium and had met Viviani, published in the *Acta eruditorium* of Leipzig a memorandum in which he put forward certain observations in favour of the movement of the earth: he was careful to specify that the sentence, considering the widespread acceptance of the heliocentric theory, had been intended to declare that it could not be considered a certain truth. It could be put forward, on the contrary, as a scientific hypothesis, which if it were to be proved true, would certainly have allowed a different interpretation of those passages of Scripture in which, according to their literal expression, the immobility of the earth and the movement of the sun were asserted. In conclusion, research into a valid and conclusive physico-mathematical demonstration of the movement of the earth should be considered perfectly licit. In Kochansky, the study of the heliocentric theory was freed from all conditioning of a theological or scriptural kind, and a corresponding freedom of scientific research was thus upheld.[226]

Towards the end of the seventeenth century and at the beginning of the eighteenth, a viewpoint of this kind about the limitations that could be recognised to the sentence was coming to be expressed. It contrasted with the traditional standpoint – by far the prevalent one in Roman church circles – and was later to inform subsequent provisions by the ecclesiastical authorities on the complex question of Galileo's teachings.[227] The greatest astronomic discovery of the century, the demonstration of the aberration of starlight by James Bradley, finally offered the physical and mathematical proof of the movement of the earth around the sun; in 1734 the Italian translation of the fifth volume of "Philosophical Transactions" gave wide publicity to the celebrated report of the British astronomer. The "official" interpretation of the sentence of 1633, for which the theory of the movement of the earth was formally heretical, could obviously be no longer sustained: this was the sense in which the anonymous theologian who had taken on the task of annotating the Roman edition (1759) of the *Biblioteca canonica, iuridica, moralis, theologica* in eight volumes by Lucio Ferraris, consultant of the Holy Office, expressed his opinion. Under the heading *haereticus*, Ferraris had stated that the sentence of 1633 had defined the heliocentric theory as heretical. In the notes it is stated, on the other hand, that the sentence could not be considered an explicit declaration of heresy with regard to the Copernican-Galilean notion, but only a ban on maintaining it and teaching it as true: *"[...] etsi enim qualificatores notarint ut in philosophia falsam et formaliter haereticam hanc propositionem [...] tamen Apostolica Sede neque tunc deinceps illam declaravit"* For this reason Galileo was not condemned as a heteric, but as "suspected of heresy"; it follows that the heliocentric notion could be maintained as a mere hypothesis. This means that if secure and conclusive proofs were to be formulated, the heliocentric theory would certainly be recognised as true, even against the traditional and literal interpretation of Scripture, which would evidently have been expressed, as far as the immobility of the earth and the movement of the sun were concerned, according to the common way of speaking about the matter.[228] Very probably, these considerations arose out of the reasoning which had inspired the provision of the Holy Office in 1741, which permitted a first complete edition of Galileo's works, including the *Dialogo*, an initiative which was taken, as we know, by the Abbot Giuseppe Toaldo, and carried out in the printing house of the Seminary of Padua. In this way the absolute ban on the *Dialogo* was brought to an end; the heliocentric theory was no longer defined as formally heretical, even though the publishers in their preface declared their full adhesion to the sentence, which was in substance contradicted by the permission of the ecclesiastical authorities to publish the work of Galileo.[229] Once the authorisation for the printing of the *Dialogo* had been granted, it made no further sense to ban books which upheld the theory of the movement of the earth: in 1757, by a decree of the Congregation of the Index, all writings which upheld the heliocentric theory were, in fact, omitted from the new Index.[230] The implicit consequence, though indirectly, was a declaration of the nullity of the essential presupposition on which the sentence of 1633 was based: that the movement of the earth was philosophically false. In this way the judgement on Galileo's behaviour and his condemnation to abjure no longer had any juridical justification. The nullity of the presupposition ended by affecting the sentence as a whole.

In 1764, the first edition of the treatise on astronomy by Jerome La Lande appeared in Paris; in it an organic exposition of the whole Copernican system was provided,[231] and the Galileo issue was taken up anew, showing how inadequate and deviant the literal interpretation of all those passages from the Bible in which mention is made of natural phenomena really was. In summing up the terms of the debate about the sentence, the scientist observed that it was the fruit of doubts and academic jealousies, of which Galileo had been a victim: "[...] but this sentence by the Inquisition against Galileo was a personal affair, a result of jealousies which his over-powerful enemies felt towards this new philosophy, and towards the extraordinary fame of Galileo".[232] On the occasion of his journey to Italy in 1765, during his stay in Rome, La Lande had a chance to call the attention of the Cardinal Prefect of the Congregation of the Index to the fact that after the decree of 1757, the works of Galileo should be removed from the Index by a specific measure. Since according to the Cardinal, the sentence of condemnation was an obstacle to any such provision, La Lande appealed to the Pope, Clement XIII, expressing the hope that there could be an examination of whether it would be appropriate to revise that condemnation in the light of new scientific findings which had confirmed the theories of Copernicus and Galileo. This was the first time, as far as I have been able to discover, that an explicit request was presented to the highest authorities of the Church for the revision of the sentence. Clement XIII, from what La Lande tells us, showed his positive interest in the question; "[…] and Pope Clement XIII […] seemed to me to be very well-disposed to give his consent, through deference to science and to men of learning […]".[233] Unfortunately the limited time of his stay in Rome and his subsequent commitments did not allow the French scientist to devote the necessary amount of time for appeal to other personalities and other Congregations, whose interest might have set in motion the complex procedure of revision of sentence – even though this had seemed possible because of the concern shown by the Pope.

La Lande's opinions, so authoritative from the scientific point of view, were not without reflection in the ecclesiastical world and in the Italin cultural scene, more directly involved in the study of Galileo's work. The Jesuit Luigi Brenna, author of a life of Galileo published by Fabroni in Pisa in 1778, had observed that after the numerous scientific discoveries, the Copernican/Galilean theory was by now universally adopted without the church authorities intervening to re-impose the old condemnation and block the spread of the relative works.[234] About ten years later, the noted scholar and man of letters, Abbot Girolamo Tiraboschi, himself a former Jesuit, thought it appropriate to insert into his famous *Storia della letteratura italiana,* with regard to the work of Galileo, two memoranda to give specific detail of some aspects of the complex procedure of the trial of Galileo.[235] The first of these, *Sui primi promotori del sistema Copernicano*, concerns the role adopted by the Church in the promotion and spread of Copernicanism, while the second refers specifically to the condemnation of Galileo. In the first, Tiraboschi documented the interest which ecclesiastical scholarship had shown in the Copernican theory, which had been welcomed, promoted and spread without any reservations of a theological kind. In fact, Nicholas Cusanus had already put forward the heliocentric theory without arousing any remonstrations; subsequently in the first half of the sixteenth century, Cardinal Schönberg, Bishop Gisio, Clement VII and Paul III had all welcomed and supported by their authority the work of Copernicus, later confirmed by the reform of the calendar undertaken by Gregory XIII. The spread and extension of the Copernican theory was thanks to Italy and the Church. This consideration, Tiraboschi notes, must guide us in studying the question of Galileo and of the scientist's condemnation. The latter was due to the fact that Galileo not only defied the ban which had been placed on him in 1616, prohibiting him from maintaining the truth of the heliocentric theory, but also provoked the impression (in several ways not unfounded) among the judges of the Inquisition that he had sought to be little the arguments in favour of the geocentric theory, presenting them as considerations dictated by presumptuous ignorance, so that Simplicius, the character to whom the defence of the geocentric system is entrusted in the *Dialogo*, became an object of general derision.[236] But after having pointed out Galileo's obstinacy and imprudence, the Jesuit does admit that "at that time too many vulgar prejudices existed in Rome, and it was these that brought about the prohibition of the Copernican system [...]".[237] Nor could it be said that "the conduct used towards Galileo was in all ways praiseworthy. Too much faith was placed on that occasion in the peripatetic philosophers, who, since they did not know how to respond to Galileo's arguments, used the authority of Scripture as a shield. There was not enough examination of whether Galileo's arguments had enough strength to render the abandonment of the literal meaning licit, and it was supposed that it had already been demonstrated that the sacred text could have no other interpretation".[238] Despite the condemnation, the strength of Galileo's arguments upholding the heliocentric theory has induced many scholars to study it in depth and augment its value by further proofs, so that "it has indeed become universal among scholars, so that no one now has the courage to follow any other opinion". It can rightly be said that "Galileo's observations (are) commonly recognised and adopted as principles on which almost all modern philosophy is founded".[239] In the light of these considerations, Tiraboschi stresses, and gives specific details of, the observation concerning the nature and limitations of the condemnation, which refers exclusively to the ban imposed by the Congregation of the Index. The Church had not expressed a judgment of heresy either about the Copernican theory, or about Galileo: "[...] I will only reflect that Galileo was not condemned by the Church Universal, nor by the Roman Church, but only by the Tribunal of the Inquisition, to whom no one, even among the most zealous theologians, has ever accorded the right of infallibility; and that thus in reflecting that the Church, even in those times, in which it was very commonly believed that the teaching of Copernicus and Galileo was contrary to Holy Scripture, yet never condemned it as heretical, teaches us to realise with what caution it proceeds in its most solemn decisions".[240] In effect, Tiraboschi, with that tact and diplomacy which Galileo had lacked, brought back the question of Galileo into the world of ecclesiastical culture, with an implicit reference to the contrast between the acceptance of the Copernican and Galilean theories – which corresponded to the original interest in them – and the sentence of condemnation by the Inquisition.

In 1820, the Congregation of the Holy Office had the opportunity to discuss the essential problem raised by the sentence of 1633: whether a principle of faith had been pronounced on that occasion, and thus whether the declaration of heresy in the case of the movement of the earth was irreversible. The Master of the Sacred Palace, Filippo Anfossi, had declared himself to be of this opinion: he had denied the *Imprimatur* to the *Elementi di ottica e di astronomia* by Canon Settele, who taught this subject at the La Sapienza University in Rome. Settele then appealed to the Pope, Pius VII, who referred the question back to the Congregation of the Index. After the examination of the question, permission to publish was granted. Another refusal by the Master of the Sacred Palace; he maintained that in fact in the sentence of 1633 a principle of faith had been declared, which could not be changed even by the Pope himself, and stated that he could not subscribe to the decision of the Congregation of the Index, and so again refused the granting of the *Imprimatur*.[241]

The question was then passed on to the Congregation of the Holy Office, and by an irony of fate, the Master of the Sacred Palace ran the risk of suffering a judgment by the Inquisition for his strenuous defence of the theory of the immobility of the earth. On that occasion, the whole affair of the Galileo question was re-examined on the basis of the decrees of 1616 and 1633, the sentence, and the subsequent provisions of 1741 and 1757. From the documents consulted, the file on the actual trial was missing; as mentioned it was only restored to the Holy See in 1843. It was specified that the sentence had examined and judged the Copernican question on the basis of the scientific knowledge of the time, without any preclusion of future discoveries and proofs of the heliocentric theory; by the term 'heresy' it was intended to indicate the non-conformity of the Copernican and Galilean theory with the constant and traditional interpretation of certain passages of Scripture, but not the violation of a principle of faith, which, as had been maintained in previous interpretations of the sentence, had never been defined. In effect, the physical and astronomical discoveries made and the latest scientific proofs demonstrated during the last century had confirmed the heliocentric system, while, as regards the passages of Scripture, a more profound and certain knowledge of ancient Jewish history made it possible to understand the relationship between the Hebrew cosmological view and the terms and expressions and the expressions which had been used in the Biblical text. In the meeting of 16th August 1820, the Cardinals of the Congregation of the Holy Office *"lecto voto R.P.M. Antonii Mariae Grandi, [...] decreverunt iuxta votum P. Consultoris qui scripsit nempe: Nihil obstare, quominus defendi possit sententia Copernici de motu telluris eo modo quo nunc ab auctoribus Catholicis defendi solet".*[242]

The sentence of 1633 was thus substantially and finally 'annulled': the intention of Galileo, his profound conviction that no opposition existed between the new natural science and the Word, that one could demonstrate the truth of the Copernican theory without bringing down the principles of faith, was just, Catholic, in conformity with "the way it is customary to defend it among Catholic authors"; he was in fact a Catholic author because he had always been so. It was also recognised that the accusation of heresy was non-existent: the trial *de vehementi haeresis suspicione*, the condemnation to a solemn abjuration which so greatly afflicted him, now appeared as a veritable "excess of power". This, basically, was the reason for the reservations, the perplexities, the difficulties to which Maculano had referred, and above all for the non-signing of the sentence on the part of three cardinals.[243] The trial had been resolved for Galileo into the tormented experience of the "temptation of thought", which arose out of his profound faith in the truth of the Church, and out of his intimate conviction of natural truth: the former rejected the latter, and imposed the error. Galileo won the "temptation";[244] he did not reduce the truth of the Church to that of science, nor did he declare himself to be fully satisfied with the latter alone: the abjuration, paradoxically, allowed him solemnly to reaffirm his wish to remain within the Church, to recognise the Church as truth, and to declare the honesty and sincerity of his intentions, which even so excluded his personal adhesion to the precept that the Ptolemaic theory must be held to be the truth: "[…] he besought the Lords Cardinals that, since he had been dealt with in this manner, they might cause him to say whatever their Eminences wished, except for just two things: the one, that he should never be forced to say that he was not a Catholic, for such he was, and so he wished to die, to the shame and disgrace of his ill-wishers; the other was that he could not say that he had ever deceived anyone, and especially over the publication of the book […] after which affirmation, he read out what Fr Firenzuola had spread before him".[245] Thus he reaffirmed the sincerity of his faith in the Church; he witnessed by his abjuration, and by the humiliation which caused him so much affliction, that for a Catholic the truth of the Church was the presupposition for the truth of science. This is certainly one of the highest testimonies of the modern Catholic conscience.

Notes

1 On Galileo's "rhetorical skill" see J. Dietz Moss: *Galileo's Rhetorical Strategies in Defence of Copernicanism*, in *Novità celesti e crisi del sapere*, Atti del Convegno Internazionale di studi galileiani, edited by P. Galluzzi, Florence 1984, pp. 95-103.

2 For the history of the events related to the transfer of the manuscript containing the papers of the trial, and its restitution to the Holy See, see A. FAVARO, *Documenti per la storia del processo originale di Galileo*, in *Miscellanea galileiana inedita. Studi e ricerche*, Venice, 1887, pp. 178-228; A. MERCATI: *Come e quando ritornò a Roma il codice del processo di Galileo*, in «Atti della Pontificia Accademia delle Scienze, Nuovi Lincei», LXXX, session of 19-12-1926, Rome 1927. The manuscript was not returned when the Holy See recovered the Archives of the Holy Office in 1817, and it was kept by Count Blacas d'Aulps, who during the revolution of 1830 followed Charles X into exile. After his death his widow found the manuscript in the family archive, and following her husband's instructions, she restored it to the Holy See in 1843 through the mediation of the Nuncio in Vienna, Ludovico Altieri, who transmitted the invaluable «file» in October 1843 to the Secretary of State, Cardinal Lambruschini. The manuscript is preserved today in the Secret Archives of the Vatican. For a detailed analysis of the events relating to the restoration of the manuscript record of the trial, see S. M. PAGANO: *Introduction*, in *I documenti del processo di Galileo Galilei*, edited by S. M. Pagano, with the collaboration of A.G.Luciani, Pontificia Academia Scientiarum, Vatican City 1984, pp. 16-24.

3 The return of the manuscript permitted the first studies of the acts of the legal process, and the subsequent publication, first of a part and then of all of the documents concerning the trials of 1616 and 1633: extracts from the trials were provided by Mons. M. MARINI: *Galileo e l'Inquisizione. Memorie storico-critiche dirette alla romana Accademia di Archeologia*, Rome 1850: Marini had directed the mission to Paris for the recovery of the Vatican Archives, causing, unfortunately and thanks to incompetence, the

dispersion of important series of documents from the Archives of the Holy Office (see L. FIRPO, *Il processo di Galileo*, in *Nel quarto centenario della nascita di Galileo Galilei*, Pubblicazioni dell'Università Cattolica di Milano 1966, pp. 86-88). The choice of documents and the distinct tone of an apologia of this essay aroused the criticism of Renan (1866), who stressed the appropriateness of the publication of the whole «file» on the trial, knowledge of which was essential to form an objective judgment on the event. H. DE L'EPINOIS, *Galilée, son procès, sa condamnation d'après les documents inédits*, Paris 1867, provided further documents; a few years later S. Gherardi, who was Minister of Education in the government of the Roman republic and who had been able to consult the papers of the Archive of the Inquisition, gave further and more specific information on the acts of the trial: *Il processo di Galileo riveduto sopra documenti di nuova fonte* in «Rivista europea», 1870, III fasc. 1 pp. 3-37; fasc. 3 pp. 398-410. The various editions of the manuscript then followed: H. DE L'EPINOIS, *Les pieces du procès de Galilée*, Rome-Paris 1877; K. VON GEBLER, *Galileo Galilei unt die römische Curie nach den autentischen Quellen*, Stuttgart 1876; Idem: *Die Acten des Galileischen Processes. Nach der Vaticanischen handschrift*, Stuttgart 1877, translated into Italian, *Galileo Galilei e la Curia Romana*, Italian transaltion by G. Prato, Florence 1879, vols. I-II; D. BERTI, *Il processo originale di Galileo Galilei*, Rome 1878, 2nd editing, 1893; A. WOLINSKY, *Nuovi documenti inediti del processo di Galilei*, Florence 1878; *Galileo e l'Inquisizione. Documenti del processo galilaeiano esistenti nell'Archivio del S. Ufficio e nell'Archivio Segreto Vaticano per la prima volta integralmente pubblicati da* A. FAVARO, Florence, 1907: is the most careful editing of the acts of the trial, which was later included in Vol. XIX of the national Editing of the works of Galileo (Ed. Naz.). A new edition of the acts of the trial which takes account of Favaro's work, and made use of further finds in the Archives of the Holy Office and the Vatican Secret Archives, has been promoted by the Pontifical Academy of Science and by the Vatican Archive, *I documenti del processo di Galileo Galilei* op. cit.

4   A. GEMELLI, *Scienza e fede nell'uomo Galilei*, in *Nel terzo centenario della morte di Galileo Galilei*, Publications of the Catholic University of the Sacred Heart, Milan, 1942, p. 2. For a detailed examination of the theological and philosophico-scientific implications of the Galileo question in the light of the recent historiographical standpoints, see D. GALATI, *Galileo, Primario matematico e filosofo*, Rome 1991.

5   E.A. BURTT, *The metaphysical Foundation of modern physical science*, Garden City, 1955, page 38.

6   Bacon's judgments on the Copernican system to which we are referring here were expressed in *Novum Organum* (1620) and in *De dignitate et augmentis scientiarum* (1623, see F. BACON, Works, ed. J. Spedding., R. L. Ellis and D. D. Heath, London 1870, I, pp. 297-298, 551-552. On the Baconian conception of astronomy with particular reference to Copernicus see the Preface by J. SPEDDING to the *Descriptio Globi intellectuallis* (published posthumously in 1653) in Works III, pp. 715-726. On the relations of Bacon with Copernicus and Galileo, see further P. ROSSI, *Venti, maree, ipotesi astronomiche in Bacone e in Galilei,* in Various, *Aspetti della rivoluzione scientifica,* Naples 1971, pp. 153-157, in particular on Bacon as astronomer, pp. 198-201; Idem: *Galileo e Bacone,* in *Saggi su Galileo Galilei,* collected and published under the editorship of C. Maccagni, Florence 1972, pp. 248-296.

7   G. GALILEI, *Dialogo dei massimi sistemi,* in *Le opere di Galileo Galilei,* Edizione Nazionale, Florence 1890-1909, VII, p. 355.

8   N. COPERNICUS, *Le rivoluzioni delle sfere celesti,* in *Opere,* edited by F. Barone, Turin 1979, p. 177, and notes 20-21; A. KOESTLER, *I sonnambuli. Storia delle concezioni dell'universo,* Italian translation by G. Giacometti, Milan, 1981, p. 144.

9   A MÜLLER, *Niccolò Copernico. Fondatore dell'astronomia moderna,* Italian translation by P. Mazzetti, Rome, 1902, pp. 106-107; E. COSTANZI, *La Chiesa e la dottrina copernicana,* Siena 1898, pp. 86-87; A. KOESTLER: *I sonnambuli,* op. cit., p. 150.

10   N. COPERNICUS, *Opere,* op. cit., p. 845.

11   D. BERTI, *Copernico e le vicende del sistema copernicano,* Rome, 1876, p. 155; A. MÜLLER, *Niccolò Copernico,* op. cit., pp. 109-110; E. COSTANZI, *La Chiesa e la dottrina copernicana,* op. cit., pp. 166-167; T. S. KUHN, *La rivoluzione copernicana,* Italian translation by T. Gaino, Turin, 1972, pp. 245-252.

12   N. COPERNICUS, *Opere,* op. cit., pp. 176-178.

13   G. G. RETICO, *Esposizione dei libri delle rivoluzioni,* in N. COPERNICUS, *Opere,* op. cit., pp. 771-786, 831-835. The information about the small work of Retico in defence of the Copernican theory is provided for us by the letter of Bishop Giese, in N. COPERNICUS, *Opere,* op. cit., p. 847.

14   On the relations between Copernicus and Osiander, see F. BARONE in N. COPERNICUS, *Opere,* op. cit., pp. 157-161; A. KOESTLER, *I sonnambuli,* op. cit., p. 162-170.

15 On this point, especially important for the Copernican conception of astronomy and for the corresponding position of Galileo, we refer to the just considerations of F. BARONE, in N. COPERNICUS, *Opere,* op. cit., pp. 43-56, which stress the "cosmological" commitment of Copernicus, aimed at overcoming the traditional distinction between natural and mathematical philosophers, based on the conviction that through mathematics it was not possible to arrived at the knowledge of natural truth.

16 A. KOESTLER, *I sonnambuli,* op.cit., p. 170, note 60.

17 Tycho Brahe to Galileo, 4-5-1600, in Ed. Naz., X, p. 79. The arguments in favour of the new system and the criticisms of that of Copernicus had been set out by Brahe in the *Epistolarum astronomicarum libri,* 1596; W. R. SHEA, *La rivoluzione intellettuale di Galileo,* Italian translation by P. Galluzzi, Florence 1974, pp. 143-144; on the relationship between Copernicus and Brahe see T. S. KUHN, *La rivoluzione copernicana,* op. cit., pp. 256-264.

18 P. PASCHINI, *Vita e opere di Galileo Galilei,* preface by M. Maccarrone, Rome 1965, pp. 34-38. The work by Paschini is still today the broadest and most complete intellectual biography of Galileo, written with a keen historical sense, philological scruple, and respect for sources. Written at the request of Fr. Agostino Gemelli – President of the Pontifical Academy of Sciences – between 1942 and 1944, on the occasion of the third centenary of the death of Galileo, it was not published because of some reservations on the part of the Holy Office. The *Vita e opere di Galileo Galilei* was only published eventually in 1964, two years after the author's death (14-2-1962), on the occasion of the second Vatican Council, after the go-ahead was given by the Holy Office. Thanks to the intervention of the Presidency of the Pontifical Academy of Science, the responsibility for revising the text was entrusted to the Jesuit Edmond Lamalle, both for bibliographical updating and for a survey of the questions of a scientific nature in the light of the conclusions which had been reached by the historians of science. In effect, the revision, the criteria for which are indicated in Lamalle's introduction prefaced to the first edition, has a bearing also on the judgments expressed by Paschini about the responsibility for the condemnation of Galileo, to the extent that on certain issues these are modified, sometimes radically so. On the events surrounding the editing and publishing of the *Vita,* see M. MACCARRONE, *Mons. Paschini e la Roma ecclesiastica* in «Atti del Convegno di studi su Pio Paschini nel centenario della nascita (1878-1978)», Deputazione di storia patria del Friuli, 1979, pp. 99-93; P. NONIS,

L'ultima opera di Paschini: Galilei, ibid., pp. 158-172; which reveals the inappropriateness of the measure relating to the ban on publication. P. BERTOLLA, *Le vicende del "Galileo" di Paschini (dall'Epistolario Paschini-Vale)*, ibid., pp. 173-208, which apart from a detailed enquiry into the events of the composition and revision of *Galileo*, also provides indications of the «interpolations» of the reviser as compared with Paschini's original text. For a systematic re-thinking of the whole matter, see P. SIMONCELLI, *Storia di una censura, «Vita di Galileo» e Concilio Vaticano II*, Milan 1992; T. S. KUHN, *La rivoluzione copernicana*, op. cit., pp. 240-241.

19   Ed. Naz., II, pp. 198-202; see also W. R. SHEA, *La rivoluzione intellettuale di Galileo*, op.cit., pp. 145-147.

20   Ed. Naz., X, pp. 67-68. On the relations between Galileo and Keppler, see C. CHEVALLEY, *Kepler et Galilée dans la bataille du «Sidereus Nuncius» (1610-1)* in *Novità celesti e crisi del sapere*, op. cit., pp. 167-175.

21   Ed. Naz., X, p. 70; A. KOESTLER: *I sonnambuli*, op. cit., pp. 350-354. P. PASCHINI, *Vita,* op. cit., pp. 81-83.

22   F. ZAGAR, *Galileo astronomo, Fortuna di Galileo*, Bari 1964, pp. 40-41.

23   Ed. Naz., XI, pp. 22-24: «Displicet mihi, libellum tuum, antequam Methafisicos absolverem, non vidisse. Sed bene ibi docui, longe plura systemata in caelo latere quam pateant, et constructionem universi possibilem esse iuxta Coperniceas hypotheses, sed in pluribus ipsum falli, quia partim ex Pithagoreis, partim ex Ptholomaicis, in suis libris accepit, quae profeto consona non sunt [...] Gaudeamus: si murmuraverint teologi, prophetizantes defendent te patres theologiae, Chrysostomus et Theodorus episcopus Tarsensis magister eius, et Procopius Gazeus, qui caelum stare, praesertim supremum, et stellas circumvolvi, docent; et Augustinus hanc opinionem suo tempore a mathematicis rite demonstratam fuisse docet, neque per Sacras Literas evertendam esse nobis, ne simus irrisui mathematicis; quod debuisset ipse observare, cum antipodas negavit. Habes Origenem, qui terram esse animal et siderea omnia docuit, et Pithagorica dogmata laudat et ex Scripturis probat». Galileo was later to take up the reference to St Augustine in his *Lettera a Madama Cristina.*

24   Ed. Naz., X, p. 500.

25   Ed. Naz., XI, p. 12.

26   Ed. Naz., XI, p. 48.

27 Ed. Naz., V, pp. 99-100, 195.

28 Ed. Naz., XI, p. 89.

29 P. PASCHINI, *Vita,* op. cit., pp. 221-227.

30 *Contro il moto della terra,* by LUDOVICO DELLE COLOMBE, Ed. Naz., III, pp. 253-290.

31 Ed. Naz., XI, pp. 152-154.

32 Ed. Naz., XI, p. 100.

33 Ed. Naz., XI, pp. 241-242. Urged by his friends, Galileo thought it the right moment to put questions on the Copernican question to Cardinal Conti, whom he had met in Rome in 1611, with the additional aim of sounding out the thinking of the Curia. In July 1612, Conti had replied without expressing a specific condemnation of the Copernican system, and letting it be understood that the question could be examined without preconceptions: «[...] and this was the opinion of the Pythagoreans, later followed by Copernicus, by Calcagninus and others, and it does seem to be less in conformity with the Scriptures, because, although in those places where it is said that the earth is stable and stationary it can be understood to mean the perpetuity of the earth [...] even so, where it is said that the sun turns and the heavens move, the Scripture cannot have any other interpretation, except that it speaks in the common parlance of the time; this manner of interpretation cannot be admitted without great necessity. Nevertheless, Diego Stunica, writing on the ninth chapter of Job, verse 6°, says that it is more true to Scripture to say that the earth moves, even though his interpretation is not commonly followed». Ed. Naz., XI, pp. 354-355; cf. P. PASCHINI, *Vita,* op. cit., p. 285; G. DE SANTILLANA, *Processo a Galileo. Studio storico critico,* Italian translation by G. Cardona - A. Abetti, Milan 1960, pp. 74-76.

34 On the relations between Galileo and Agucchi (nephew of Cardinal Sega, Secretary of Cardinal Aldobrandini on the occasion of his missions to Florence and to Paris, who ended his ecclesiastical career as nuncio to Venice from 1624 to 1632, the year of his death) see A. FAVARO, *Amici e corrispondenti di Galileo,* edited with an introductory note by P. Galluzzi, Florence, 1983, I, pp. 373-395.

35 Ed. Naz., XI, p. 532-535.

36 Ed. Naz., XI, p. 590. On B. Castelli, see A. FAVARO, *Amici e corrispondenti di Galileo,* op. cit., Vol. II, pp. 741-838.

37 Ed. Naz., XI, pp. 605-606.

38 Ed. Naz., V, pp. 281-288.

39 The episode that gave Baronio the opportunity to express his judgment on the relationship between science and Scripture is recorded by Galileo himself in his *Lettera a Madama Cristina,* Ed. Naz., V, p. 319.

40 Ed. Naz., XII, pp. 241.242. Guicciardini further states: «[...] and if this follows only for the satisfaction of Galileo, he is passionately involved therein and, as if it were a thing of his own, does not distinguish or perceive that it would be necessary, as he has done up to now, that he would remain embroiled in it, and will bring himself into danger, and everyone who backs up his wish or lets himself be persuaded by him to do those things that he wants [...] And if Galileo awaits here for the Lord Cardinal, and intrigues in these negotiations, it will be something that will cause much displeasure, and he is vehement and stubborn and passionate on the matter, so that it is impossible for anyone around him to escape from his hands». Guicciardini had already expressed his «irritation» with regard to Galileo; he did not want trouble with the Roman Curia, especially over questions of little account from the political standpoint. Thus, basically he was advising reasons of State. He had written to C. Picchena, the Grand Duke's Chancellor: «His teaching, and certain other things do not show tact whether it be to the *Consultori and Cardinals of the Holy Office*, and among other *Bellarmine* said to me that the greatest respect must be shown to these Serene Highnesses, but that he may have been here too much, he could not do without providing some justification for his case [...] I do not know whether he has changed I doctrine or humour; I know, however, *that* certain *friars of San Domenico* who have a major role in the *Holy Office*, and others, bear him great ill will; and this is not a country to come and dispute about the moon, nor to wish in the current century to uphold nor introduce new doctrines», Ed. Naz., XII, p. 207. The Tuscan ambassador thus expressed a judgment which ended up by attributing to Galileo the responsibility for having revived the Copernican question and having insisted on the theological aspects, thus forcing the ecclesiastical authorities to intervene. Galileo seems to have lacked prudence throughout the venture driven on by his proud claim to have his opinions triumph. It is due, therefore, to the insistent propaganda in favour of Copernicus, moreover not upheld by effective proofs, that the Copernican thesis was condemned. Even Kepler, after learning the news that his *Epitome astronomiae copernicanae* had been placed on the Index (1619) lamented that the Copernican question had been inappropriately debated «coram populo», without that reserve that must characterise scientific research: «[...] because of the fact that causes the inappropriate attitude of certain who

have dealt with astronomic truths in inappropriate places and with incorrect methods, the reading of Copernicus was banned without being first amended, while for eighty years it was quite freely allowed», cf. P. PASCHINI, *Vita*, op. cit., p. 354. This notion was resumed by those who sought to justify the intervention of the ecclesiastical authorities and the condemnation, on the basis of the consideration that if Galileo was right «in substance» he was nevertheless in error «in form» i.e. in the claim that a conviction, rooted in tradition and in common experience, should be recognised in solemn fashion as being destitute of any foundation, without further confirmation of his thesis. In 1678, the Jesuit mathematician Antonio Baldigiani, to whom Viviani had turned for the possibility of a revision of the condemnation expressed this judgment: «I would add that the words: *qui si in nonnullis*, do not express in what it was lacking, if greater caution were to be used in the doctrine or in the manner of proposing it. This is termed transferring the matter from the criminal to the civil [...] This passage alludes to another which I managed to get Bartoli to insert into the *Life of Bellarmine*, as he did, even though not entirely as I wanted, where speaking of Bellarmine in relation to Galileo, he says that the Cardinal wished him well, and esteemed him highly (and I have seen some original letters to this effect), and advised him to act with greater caution, and that Galileo couldn't bring himself to make use of this advice, that if, while holding on to all of his doctrine, he should modify the manner in which it was written, then he would not have encountered that distaste, etc.. So in fact Galileo is no longer condemned for his teaching, nor is it even said that it is heresy against scripture, and of doubtful faith, but it is only the way in which it is written that is in dispute, which is a very different question from the former», see A. FAVARO, *Sulla pubblicazione della sentenza contro Galileo e sopra alcuni tentativi del Viviani di far revocare la condanna dei dialoghi galileiani,* in *Miscellanea galileiana inedita,* op. cit., pp. 143-144. A similar theory is upheld by Leibniz, who even took initiatives among Italian scholars for the revocation of the condemnation: «Fathers Mersenne, Minime and Fr Honoré Fabry, Jesuits, have recognised and taught in their writings that the ban was merely provisional, until things were made more clear, and that it was judged convenient in those days, to avoid a scandal, that this teaching, then expanded by Galileo, seemed to be born in the spirit of the weak [...]», see A. MÜLLER, *Niccolò Copernico*, op. cit., p. 179. For this historiographical line of interpretation, see also S. PIERALISI, *Urbano VIII e Galileo Galilei*, Rome, 1875, pp. 56-58; E. COSTANZI, *La Chiesa e la dottrina copernicana,* op. cit., pp. 350-351; A. MÜLLER, *Niccolò Copernico*, op.

cit., p. 157-163; Id., *Galileo Galilei. Studio scientifico,* Italian translation by P. Perciballi, preface by card. P. Maffi, Rome, 1911, pp. 139-143; J. BRODRICK, *Robert Bellarmin, l'humaniste et le saint,* Italian translation by J. Boulangé, Montreal, 1963, p. 276, who here notes it with critical reservations in Galileo's favour; M. VIGANÒ, *Il mancato dialogo tra Galileo e i teologi,* Rome, 1969, pp. 93-94. Recently this theory has been taken up again and carried to the most extreme consequences by A. KOESTLER: *I Sonnambuli,* op. cit., pp. 434-444, 492, with a concluding judgment which gives rise to reservations and perplexities, since Galileo had indicated he right solution, from the Catholic point of view, of the relation between science and faith: «[...] the "dangerous adulations" thus ended, as did one of the most disastrous episodes in the history of ideas, in as much as the rash crusade of Galileo had discredited the heliocentric system, and precipitated the divorce between science and faith». For a critical assessment of Koestler's view, see A. DE SANTILLANA, *Processo a Galileo,* op. cit., pp. 111-13; G. MORPURGO TAGLIABUE, *I processi a Galileo e l'epistemologia,* Rome 1981, pp. 155-162; for a further broad example of the judgments of Koestler on the events concerning Galileo in the light of recent historiographical debate, see J. AGASSI, *On explaining the Trial of Galileo,* in «Organon», 1971, pp. 137-166.

41 Ed. Naz., XII, p. 212.

42 Ed. Naz., XII, p. 226-227.

43 Ed. Naz., XIX, p. 297; *I documenti ,* op. cit., pp. 69-71.

44 Ed. Naz., XIX, p. 305.

45 Ed. Naz., XIX, pp. 308-309; *I documenti,* op. cit., p. 82. On the Galileo-Caccini affair, see A. RICCI, *Galileo Galilei e fra Tommaso Caccini,* Florence 1902. On this first stage of the process, see F. FLORA, *Il processo di Galileo, Narrato da F.F.,* in V. VIVIANI, *Vita di Galileo,* Milan 1854, pp. 77-85.

46 A. C. CROMBIE, *Histoire des sciences de Saint Augustin à Galilée,* Translation by J. D'Hermies, Paris 1959, pp. 47-48.

47 St AUGUSTINE, *De Genesi ad litteram,* Bk. II, Ch. 9, par. 20, PL XXXIV, col. 270.

48 St AUGUSTINE, *De Genesi ad litteram,* Bk. I, Ch. 18, par. 37; Ch. 19, par. 39, PL XXXIV, cols. 260, 261. On the cosmology of the church fathers, see P. DUHEM, *Le système du monde. Histoire des doctrines cosmologiques de Platon à Copernic,* Paris 1914, Vol. II, pp. 393-417; on St Augustine and questions of astronomy, see pp. 491-494.

[49] St AUGUSTINE, *De actis contra Felicem Manichaeum*, Bk. I, Ch. X, PL XLII, col. 525.

[50] On the relationship between the Aristotelian cosmological concept and the mathematical-geometric one of Ptolemy and the Middle Ages, see A. C. CROMBIE, *Histoire des sciences,* op. cit., pp. 66-75.

[51] St THOMAS AQUINAS, *De caelo et mundo,* Bk. II, reading 17, *Opera omnia*, XIX, Parma 1865: «Secundo considerandum est, quod circa motus planetarum quaedam anormalia, id est irregularitates apparent, prout scilicet planetae, quandoque velociores, quandoque stationarii, quandoque retrogradi videntur. Quod quidem non videtur esse conveniens coelestibus motibus; ut in supradictis patet: et ideo prius Plato hanc dubitationem Eudoxo, sui temporis Astrologo, proposuit, qui huiusmodi irregularitates conatus est ad rectum ordinem inducere ad signandos diversos motus planetis; quod etiam postremi Astrologi diversi mode facere conati sunt. Illorum autem suppositiones, quas adinvenerunt, non est necessarium esse veras: licet enim talis suppositionibus factis appareant solvere, non tamen oportet dicere has suppositiones esse veras, quia forte secundum aliquem modum nondum ab hominibus comprehensum, apparentia circa stellas salvatur: Aristoteles tamen utitur huiusmodi suppositionibus ad qualitatem motum tanquam veris». For a broad and systematic analysis of the astronomic teachings of St Thomas, see T. LITT, *Les corps célestes dans l'univers de Saint Thomas d'Aquin,* Louvain, Paris 1963, pp. 295-372, in particular on the problem of «astronomic hypotheses», pp. 342-366.

[52] St THOMAS, *Responsio ad magistrum Joannem de Vercellis de articulis XLII, Opera omnia,* XVI, p. 163.

[53] M. CANI, *Opera,* Matriti 1760, *De Locis theologicis,* Bk.VII, Chap. III, pp. 230, 269, 270; see also P. MANDONNET, *Cano Melchior* in *Dictionnaire de théologie catholique,* Paris, 1909, II (2), coll. 1537-1540.

[54] DIDACI A ZUÑICA, *In Job Commentaria,* Toledo, 1584, Ch. IX, par 5°, p. 205; for an analysis of the theses of Zuñica, see E. COSTANZI, *La Chiesa e la dottrina copernicana,* op. cit., pp. 127-132. Zuñica was mentioned by Galileo in his *Letter to Madame Christine,* together with two other theologians: Paolo di Burgos and Alfonso Tostado, bishop of Avila; on the problems of the relations between the Copernican notions and the Scriptures, see B. CARRARA, *Il sistema copernicano e la Sacra Scrittura al tempo di Galileo,* Siena 1913; ID., *La Sacra Scrittura, SS. Padri e Galileo sopra il moto della terra,* Milan 1914; a careful analysis of the theologians who commented on the passages of the Old Testament which referred to the geocentric system between 1580 and 1620, can be found in

C. M. MARTINI, *Gli esegiti del tempo di Galileo*, in *Nel quarto centenario della nascita di Galileo Galilei*, op. cit., pp. 115-124; and for a theological assessment of the exegesis by Galileo, see ID., *Galileo e la teologia*, in *Saggi su Galileo Galilei*, op. cit., pp. 441-451: «Almost three centuries of exhaustive theological and critico-literary exploration were to be needed, and the new viewpoint offered by the rediscovery of the ancient oriental literature, for Galileo's hermeneutical insights, freed from the conditioning of the era, to show the solid nucleus of truth which they contained». P. NONIS, *Galileo e la Religione*, in *Nel quarto centenario della nascita di Galileo Galilei*, op. cit., pp. 139-143. An interesting re-examination of the exegetical question, with reference to the theories of Galileo, in particolar those concernine the work of the Jesuits, see B. Pereyra, in R. FABRIS, *Galileo Galilei e gli orientamenti esegetici del suo tempo*, Pontificia Academia Scientiarum, Vittà del Vaticano, 1986, pp. 29-33.

[55] DIDACI A ZUÑICA, *In Job Commentaria*, op. cit., p. 205: «Certum est enim Ptolomeum non potuisse neque equinoctiorum motuum explicare, neque ostendere certum, et stabili anni principium, id quod ipse fatetur in tertio magnae compositionis, capite secundo, idque inveniendum relinquit in posterum ab astrologis iis qui observationes, maior quam ipse intervallo distantes, possunt comparare [...] verum tum harum rerum rationes dissertisssime ex motu terrae a Copernico declarantur et demonstrantur et reliquia omnia aptius convenire», cf. E. COSTANZI, *La Chiesa e la dottrina copernicana*, op. cit., p. 128. The two copies possessed by the National Library of Rome, from the former fund of the Jesuits, have the pages in which the Copernican notions are accepted covered with white gummed paper, which does not permit the reading of the «incriminating» passages.

[56] E. AMANN, *Pázmány Pierre*, in *Dictionnaire de la Théologie Catholique*, Paris 1932, XII, coll. 97-100; J. KORNIS, *Le Cardinal Pázmány* (1570-1637), Paris 1937.

[57] P. *Card*. PÁZMÁNY, *Opera Omnia*, t. III, *Tractatus in libro Aristotelis de coelo, de generatione et corruptione atque in libros meteorum*, rec. D. Bognar, Budapestini 1897, p. 41: «[...] quod cum astrologi tot orbes, orbiculos, epicyclos, etc., imaginantur in coelis, non idcirco id illos dicere quasi re vera sentiant» Pázmány is referring to the writing of A. PICCOLOMINI (the Sienese man of letters and scientist) *La prima parte delle Theoriche ovvero Speculationi de i pianeti*, Venice 1568, Bk. I, Ch. X, fol. 22-23. Piccolomini had already published a text on astronomy, in which he had expounded the Aristotelian-Ptolemeian

teaching, and had criticised on the basis of the Ptolemeian texts, the movement of the earth, without however making any reference to its upholders. See *La sfera del mondo,* Venice 1566, Bk. II, Chs. VII-X, pp. 43-55. To judge from the *formulae* used by the qualificators of the Holy Office, on the occasion of the 1616 trial, to condemn the heliocentric thesis, and from the corresponding pronouncements of Piccolomini, the theory may be put forward that both Caccini and the churchmen called to express their opinion had derived their astronomic information from *La sfera del mondo.*

58 P. PÁZMÁNY, *Tractatus,* op. cit., pp. 65-70.

59 P. PÁZMÁNY, *Tractatus,* op. cit., p. 71.

60 The interest aroused by the work of the Congregation instituted, apparently in 1572, by Gregory XIII for the reform of the calendar, because of the commitment which this Pope showed to bringing to a conclusion the reform, actuated by the Apostolic Letter *Inter gravissima* of 24th February 1582, brought the Copernican theories expounded in the *De revolutionibus* back to the attention not only of mathematicians and astronomers but also to ecclesiastical circles more directly involved in the reform of the calendar. In this way a cultural mindset found expression, especially in the context of the Jesuits of the Collegio Romano. They were particularly interested in the astronomical work of Copernicus, and the conviction became widespread, given credence by the authority of Clavius, that the astronomical calculations of Copernicus had permitted that reform of the calendar, which had been hoped for and requested since the second half of the thirteenth century: this notion was upheld, as we have seen, by Zuñica, and later taken up in the midst of the polemic over Galileo, by Campanella in his *Apologia pro Galilaeo* and in the letter to Urban VIII of June 1628: «For in truth it was necessary to hold to Copernicus, because the reform of the calendar gives true and powerful witnesses to his observations and not his opinions». A proof of the interest in Copernicus aroused in the years 1570-1590 by the reform of the calendar is to be found in a copy of the *De revolutionibus*, in the Basle edition of 1566, donated by St Luiz Gonzaga to the Library of the Collegio Romano in the years of his Roman novitiate, and at present preserved in the National Library in Rome under the catalogue no. 71-2-E-23. This gift, preserved in its time in the secret section of the Jesuit library, is a clear sign of the cultural interest, or rather of the «intellectual curiosity» of one of the most famous alumni of those years in the Collegio Romano, who, it should be remembered, had Bellarmine as his spiritual director. On the reform of the Gregorian Calendar, see the Acts of the International

Conference for the celebration of the 400th anniversary of the Gregorian Calendar: *Gregorian reform of the Calendar. Proceedings of the Vatican Conference to commemorate its 400th Anniversary, 1582-1982*, edited by G. V. COYNE, S. J., M. A. HOSKIN and O. PEDERSEN, Pontificia Accademia Scientiarum-Specola Vaticana, Città del Vaticano, 1983; on the history of the calendar see J. D. NORTH, *The Western Calendar. «Intolerabilis, Horribilis et Derisibilis». Four Centuries of Discontent*, pp. 75-113; on the contribution of Copernicus to the reform, see J. D.NORTH, *op. cit.*, pp. 98-99; J. DOBRZYCKI, *Astronomical Aspects of the Calendar reform*, pp. 122-125; E. PROVERBIO, *Copernicus and the Determination of the Length of the tropical Year*, pp. 129-133; on the relations between Clavius and Copernicus, see U. BALDINI, *Christophorus Clavius and the Scientific Scene in Rome*, pp. 150-154.

61 P. A. FOSCARINI, *Sopra l'opinione de' Pittagorici e del Copernico nella quale si accordano e si appaciano i luoghi della Sacra Scrittura e le riproposizioni teologiche che possono addursi contro di tale opinione*, in G. GALILIEI, *Opere*, Firenze, 1846, t. V, pp. 455-514; for the scheme of the writing see letter from Foscarini to Galileo, Ed. Naz., XII, pp. 215-220.

62 Ed. Naz., XII, pp. 216-217.

63 Ed. Naz., XII, pp. 154, 165.

64 It is Campanella himself who records this detail in a passage from his *Quaestiones physicae,* Paris 1637, q. X, art. 4, 106; on the relationship between the philosopher and Galileo see R. AMERIO, *Galileo e Campanella: la tentazione del pensiero nella filosofia della Riforma cattolica,* in *Nel terzo centenario della morte di Galileo Galilei,* op. cit., pp. 299-325; A. CORSANO, *Campanella e Galileo,* in «Giornale Critico della filosofia italiana», Florence 1965, pp. 313-332; T. CAMPANELLA, *Apologia di Galileo,* edited by S. Femiano, Milan 1971, pp. 19-30. On the charge by Cardinal Castani to Campanella to give an opinion on the question under examination in the Holy Office, the interpreters do not agree: Amabile and Firpo hold that this is an «inventino» of the philosopher, who knew he had to be careful about calling an illustrious churchman into the case – and one who, having died in 1617, could no longer deny the matter. Amerio and Feminao, on the other hand, on the basis of the repeated declarations by the philosopher and the witness of the actual correspondence with Galileo, hold that in effect the Cardinal did request Campanella for an opinion on the Galileo question. We know from other sources that Caetani was contrary to the Copernican theses being declared heretical, and that he intervened in this direction, in agreement

with Maffeo Barberini and Bellarmine; in the absence of any document which actually witnesses to the request to Campanella, the coincidence should be pointed out between Caetani's way of thinking and the opinion expressed by Campanella, which, as witness the letter of Failla to Galileo of September 1616, was then sent on to the Cardinal.

[65] T. CAMPANELLA, *Apologia di Galileo*, op. cit., p. 70.

[66] *Ibid.*, p. 73.

[67] *Ibid.*, p. 51.

[68] *Ibid.*, p. 80.

[69] *Ibid.*, pp. 82, 83-84.

[70] Ed. Naz., XI, p. 93; on the relations between Galileo and the mathematicians of the Collegio Romano, the essay by P. M. D'ELIA, *Galileo in Cina. Relazioni attraverso il Collegio Romano tra Galileo e I gesuiti scienzati missionari in Cina,* Rome 1947, is especially important. It is based on previously unpublished documents which clarify the scientific attitudes of some members of the Collegio, for the period 1590-1616. From these documents we discover not only the very lively interest in Galileo's discoveries, but also in the Copernican system, defended within the Order by Wenceslao Kirvitzer (pp. 32-39). On the relations between Grienberger and Galileo, pp. 18-20. It should be remembered that in those years, the naturalist of the Academy of the Lincei, G. Schreck, had entered the Jesuit Order: he always showed great respect to the theories of Galileo. See also, R. G. VILLOSLADA, *Storia del Collegio Romano dal suo inizio (1551) alla soppressione della Compagnia di Gesù (1773)*, Rome 1954, pp. 194-213.

[71] C. CLAVIO, *Opera Matematica,* t. III, Mainz 1611, p. 75; see also P. M. D'ELIA, *Galileo in Cina,* op. cit., p. 14. In the *Letter to Madame Christine* Galileo had made an implicit appeal to the mathematicians of the Collegio Romano, in particular to Clavio: «I could also name to you other mathematicians, who, moved by my latest discoveries, have confirmed that it is necessary to change the received constitution of the world, as it can no longer stand on any count». Ed. Naz., V, p. 328; the manuscript copy of the letter carries in the margin in Galileo's hand the note: «Clavius». Another admirer of Galileo was the Jesuit, Gregorio di Saint Vincent.

[72] Ed. Naz., XII, p. 181.

[73] Bellarmine had studied astronomy in depth, and was by no means «wanting in such matter», as Galileo on the other hand asserted, see U. BALDINI, *L'astronomia del Cardinale Bellarmino,* in *Novità celesti e crisi*

del sapere, op. cit., pp. 293-305; he had taught astronomy in the Jesuit colleges of Florence and Mondovì, very probably making use of the *Sfera* of A. Piccolomini, which refers to the heliocentric theory without mentioning Copernicus, criticising it on the basis of Tycho's arguments.

74   The parts of the *Lectiones Lovanienses* which refer to the cosmological conception have been published in «Studi galileiani dell'Osservatorio Vaticano»: *The Louvain Lectures (Lectiones Lovanienses) of Bellarmine and the Autograph Copy of his 1616 Declaration to Galileo. Texts in the Original Latin (Italian) with English Translation, Introduction, Commentary and Notes* by U. BALDINI and G. V. COYNE, S. J., Specola Vaticana, Vatican City 1984: the authors show how Bellarmine had criticised the Aristotelian conception of the heavens, and certain aspects of the spherical astronomy before the appearance of the Nova of November 1572, which by the way poses the problem of the revision of the Aristotelian theories of the incorruptibility of the heavens, pp. 3-5. In Question 69 «de opere tertiae diei» Bellarmine examines the «3m Dub. an sol, et stellae sint fixae in coelo, et moveantur ad motum coeli, vel moveantur per se coelo quiescente», *op. cit.,* pp. 19-21. Bellarmine favours the opinion that the stars move of their own motion, in the same manner as the planets, whose movements, as is known, do not appear uniform to our observations. He recalls that various theories have been formulated to explain this phenomenon, and that there is no agreement among astronomers to indicate a single solution: «Et idcirco dum inter astrologos durat lis, sicut vere adhuc durat, de modo explicandi huiusmodi apparentias. Nam alii explicant per motum terrae, et quietem omnium stellarum; alii per quaedam figmenta epicyclorum et excentricorum; alii per motum syderum a se ipsis». In this situation, according to Bellarmine, the interpreter of Scripture must follow three criteria: it was not the task of the theologian to carry out a close investigation of astronomic questions, the study of which was properly the task of astronomy («Ad theologum non spectat hae diligenter investigare»); theology does not enter into the scientific merit of the solutions or hypotheses proposed, nor does it judge them or discuss them from the scientific standpoint. The task of the theologian, on the other hand (second criterion) is to choose the explanation «most in conformity» with Scripture, i.e. which better than others clarifies and explains the text. For this very motive, as we have seen. Diego da Zuñica had welcomed the Copernican theories in the explanation of a passage of Job. Finally, when soundly obtained and proven scientific opinions exist, it is necessary to study in what way Scripture must be rightly interpreted: «Si vero aliquando evidenter consisterit […] hoc

videndum erit quomodo recte intelligantur Scripturae [...] Certum enim est verum sensum Scripturae cum nulla alia veritate sive philosophica sive astrologica pugnare». This page from Bellarmine is inspired by the distinction between theology and science, and the recognistion of the proper context of scientific investigation, the results of which must be obtained as such; given these premises, it make no further sense to condemn or commend a scientific theory on the basis of Scripture. The passage from *Lectiones Lovanienses* has been pointed out by F. SOCCORSI, *Il processo di Galileo*, Rome 1963, pp. 37-38; see also M. VIGANÒ, *Il mancato dialogo fra Galileo e I teologi*, op. cit., p. 86; on the relations between Bellarmine and Galileo, see J. BRODRICK, *Robert Bellarmin*, op. cit., pp. 296-300; A. C. CROMBIE, *Histoire des Sciences*, op. cit., pp. 410-413.

75 The long debate on the Galileo issue and the studies of the history of science, dedicated in particular to Galileo's discoveries, have established that Galileo, in effect, had not supplied a physico-mathematical proof of the movement of the earth, of which he had given a geometrical explanation that in certain ways confirmed the findings of Tycho Brahe. Galileo held that he could prove the movement of the earth irrefutably from the tides, which would in point of fact be determined by the translocation-rotation of the earth itself. This explanation, it is now known, was erroneous. Bacon, to whom the matter had been referred in 1617, rejected it because it was not consistent with the data that were already possessed concerning the periods of the tides. The physical and mathematical proofs were only provided after the discovery of the laws of gravitation by Newton, when it was realised that since the mass of the sun was three hundred and thirty times greater than that of the earth, the latter, according to barycentric theory, could not do otherwise than rotate around the sun. Bradley, with the discovery of the aberration of light, gave a first physical proof of the Copernican theory; the determination of the stellar parallax, another physical proof of the movement of the earth, of which Galileo had written in the *Dialogo dei Massimi Sistemi*, was only demonstrated in 1837 by F. W. Bessel, who moreover followed the differential method illustrated by Galileo in the *Dialogo*. On the other hand, the arguments against the Copernican system had been expounded by Tycho Brahe, whose authority as an astronomer and an extremely scrupulous calculator conferred special credibility on his criticisms of the heliocentric theory: the letter of Mons. Agucchi should be remembered in this context. An effective synthesis of the proofs adopted by Galileo to demonstrate the heliocentric system is provided by F. SOCCORSI, *Il processo di Galileo*, op. cit., pp. 67-77; he stresses the

importance of the proof deduced from the rotatory axis of the sun, determined on the basis of the study of sun spots. A similar observation can be found in G. DE SANTILLANA, *Processo a Galileo*, op. cit., p. 652; for I. ZAGAR, *Galileo astronomo*, op. cit., pp. 67-68: «[...] the explanation by Galileo of the heliocentric system was, if not exactly a mathematical proof, certainly one of the clearest intuitive proofs that could be provided at that time»; see further, R. LENOBLE, *Histoire de la Science*, Paris 1957, pp. 473-475; A. C. CROMBIE, *Histoire des sciences*, op. cit., pp. 401-402; C. CATTANEO, *La dinamica galileiana*, in ACCADEMIA NAZIONALE DEI LINCEI, *Galileo Galilei. Le celebrazioni del IV centenario della nascita*, Rome 1965, p. 129; G. ARMELLINI, *Galilei e l'astronomia*, in *Nel terzo centenario della nascita di G. G.*, op. cit., pp. 83, 86-93; A. KOESTLER, *I sonnambuli*, Op. cit., pp. 429-431.

76 Ed. Naz., XII, pp. 171-172. On the concept of «hypothesis», around which the debate which took place in Roman ecclesiastical circles was concentrated and which was assumed as a solution of the complex Copernican question, c. f. the useful detailed examination, especially regarding astronomy, by A. KOYRÉ, *Studi newtoniani*, Italian translation by P. Galluzzi, Turin 1965, pp. 27-43, in particular the following observation, to understand the doubts that arose about the various meanings for which the word «hypothesis» was used: «It should not then be forgotten that the term "hypothesis" never has an unambiguous meaning, and assumes a whole range of meanings, moreover not easily distinguishable from each other. Common to all these definitions is the temporary (or even permanent) attenuation (or even suppression) of the affirmative character, and the reference to truth (or reality) of the hypothetical proposition», p. 34. In the hypothesis of which the astronomers from Ptolemy onwards made use, there is in effect the «definitive suppression of the affirmative character and the reference to reality», for which reason it consists in a mathematical and mental artifice, solely valid for calculating and predicting the movements of the planets, but which has no correspondence to reality; this, as we have seen, is the notion of Osiander. In St Thomas, the term «hypothesis» assumes, rather, the significance of supposition or conjecture, of which it cannot be said yet whether it be true or false, because it is not sufficiently demonstrated; it is provisional and hence probable; it may correspond or not correspond with reality. Bellarmine makes use initially, in his letter to Foscarini, of the concept of hypothesis proper to the pre-Copernican astronomers, so to speak, but then moves on when he admits that demonstration can be given of it, to the Thomistic interpretation as a probable conjecture, which may be true or false. For Galileo, on the other

hand, it has the classical significance of an «axiom» – i.e. a fundamental premise of his theories, which finds confirmation in the logico-mathematical conclusions, and since reality can be understood through numbers and the geometric forms which are its carrying structure, the hypotheses validated by demonstration are true, that is they do correspond to natural reality; the earth, with the other planets, turns around the sun, the centre of the planetary system. On the concept of hypothesis in Ballarmine see, also, A. C. CROMBIE, *Histoire des Sciences*, op. cit., pp. 410-413; for a broader discussion of the concept of hypothesis with reference to the Galileo issue, see G. MORPURGO TAGLIABUE, *I processi di Galileo e l'epistemologia*, op. cit., pp. 41-57.

77 Ed. Naz., XII, pp. 171-172. Bellarmine, from what Cesi tells us, had adopted at the beginning of the Galileo issue an attitude of clear condemnation of the Copernican thesis: «With regard to the opinion of Copernicus, Bellarmine himself, who is among the chiefs of the Congregation in these matters, told me that he considers it to be heretical, and that the movement of the earth is, without any doubt at all, contrary to Scripture [...]», Ed. Naz., XII, p. 129; in a second instance, he must have revised his stance sufficiently to agree later with Maffeo Barberini and Caetani on an intervention to avoid the Copernican thesis being declared heretical; in particular the third paragraph of the letter of Foscarini, very probably, reflects the discussion that had taken place with Grienberger, who must have pointed out to Bellarmine that there were no scientific arguments which would enable the Copernican thesis to be excluded totally, and that it seemed on the other hand to have more than one confirmation, not certain, but likely, as he had declared to Dini.

78 On the concept of «real demonstration», see U. BALDINI, *L'astronomia del Cardinale Bellarmino*, op. cit., pp. 298-300.

79 Ed. Naz., XII, p. 175.

80 Ed. Naz., XII, pp. 183-184; in *Considerazioni circa l'opinione copernicana,* written during his stay in Rome, in response to a letter from Bellarmine to Foscarini, Galileo had welcomed the observations of the Cardinal concerning the insufficiency of proofs intended to validate the heliocentric theory, thus revising the opinion expressed in his letters to Welser that his astronomic discoveries had given a sure demonstration of the Copernican system, see Ed. Naz., V, pp. 368-369: «Not to believe that there is a proof of the motion of the earth until it is shown, is the height of prudence; nor is it demanded by us that anyone shall believe such a thing without proof [...]. 7th It is true that it is not the actual showing that with

the motion of the earth and the stability of the Sun that appearances are saved, and the demonstration that such hypotheses in nature are really true; but it is quite another thing and more true that with the other commonly accepted system one cannot provide a reason for such appearances. The latter is undoubtedly false, as it is clear that the former, which is perfectly well adapted, may be true: nor can or should any other greater truth be sought for in a position, than that it responds to all appearances».

81 Ed. Naz., XII, p. 152.

82 On the relations between Galileo and Maffeo Barberini, see S. PIERALISI, *Urbano VIII e Galileo Galilei*, Rome 1875; A. FAVARO, *Oppositori di Galileo X. Maffeo Barberini,* in «Atti del R.I.V di scienze lettere ed arti», 1920-21, t. 80, p.te 2°, Venice 1921, pp. 1-46. For the Latin Ode see E. COSTANZI, *La Chiesa e le dottrine copernicane,* op. cit., pp. 437-440.

83 Ed. Naz., XII, p. 184.

84 Ed. Naz., XII, p. 146.

85 F. INGOLI, *De Situ et quiete terrae contra Copernici systema disputatio,* Ed. Naz., V, pp. 403-404, cf. P. PASCHINI, *Vita,* op. cit., p. 336.

86 A. OREGIO, *De Deo uno tractatus primus,* Rome 1629, pp. 193-194.

87 Galilean «realism» risks becoming naturalism in the sense of a mere science of quantity, the only aspect through which we can know reality. As has been rightly observed (E. AMERIO, *Epistemologia*, Brescia 1948, p. 118): «It is an easy step from affirming the quantitative aspect as what is scientifically knowable, to affirming it as the only thing that is knowable, and the only reality».

88 A. OREGIO, *De Deo uno*, op. cit., pp. 193-195: «Cum ergo Deus, quando de facto concurrit ad humanos actus, non auferat libertatem, sed illam adiuvet [...] Nam et infinita sua scientia praecognovit, quid requireretur ad hoc, ut creata voluntas posset libere operari, tam in actibus naturalibus, quam supernaturalius; et iuxta creatae voluntatis naturam, et exigentiam, uti scivit, ac potuti, sic etiam concurrere decrevit absque ullo libertatis creatae detrimento. Quod argumentum quanti faciendum sit, diligentius animadvertere incepi, dum Summus Pontifex Urbanus VIII [...] adhuc Cardinalis familiarem suum, non minus doctrina conspicuum quam religione laudabilem, admonuit, ut diligenter adverteret; An sacris conguerent scripturis, quae de motu terrae excogitaverat, ad salvanda ea omnia, quae in caelo apparent phaenomena, et quaecunque de coeli, atque astrorum motibus ex eorum diligenti inspectione et consideratione communiter recipiunt Philosophi. Concessis enim omnibus, quae Vir

doctissimus excogitaverat; quaesivit, an potuerit, et scriverit Deus alio modo disponere et movere orbes, vel sidera ita, ut quaecumque vel in caelis apparent phaenomena vel de siderum motibus, ordine, situ, distantia ac dispositione dicuntur, salvari possint. Quod si neges, Sanctissimus dixit, probare debes implicare contradictionem, posse haec aliter fieri quam excogitasti. Deus enim infinita sua potentia potest, quicquid non implicat contradictionem: cumque Dei scientia non fit minor potentia, si potuisse Deum concedimus et scivisse etiam affirmare debemus. Quod si potuti, ac novit Deus haec alio modo disponere quam excogitatum est, ita, ut salventur omnia, quae dicta sunt. Non ad hunc modum debemus divinam arctare potentiam et scientiam. Quibus auditis, quievit vir ille doctissimus». The epistemological value of the argument of Urban VIII, considered in substance as a further examination of the conception of «hypothetical» or «conventionalistic», of Osiander and Bellarmine, has been illustrated by P. DUHEM, *Essai sur la notion de théorie physique de Newton et Galilée*, in «Annales de philosophie chrétienne», 1908, pp. 584-585, 588, which defended the modernity of Bellarmine's thesis and that of Urban VIII against the dogmatic realism of Copernicus and Galileo. But it is anachronistic, as J. BRODRICK rightly observed in *Robert Bellarmin,* op. cit., p. 298: «[...] to attribute to Bellarmine and Urban VIII an exact view of scientific principles in the modern sense, and refuse such a view to Kepler and Galileo [...]». The theory of the hypothesis, as it was formulated by Maffeo Barberini, in effect posed the problem of the actual limits of the new science of nature, and has its content of truth as a warning about «scientism», of the risk or the temptation to resolve philosophy in science. It implicitly states that it is not possible to give a demonstration of «real nature», and hence of the truth (ultimate ratio, essence) of the movement of the earth, but does not deny the possibility of a demonstration of the «de facto truth» of the movement of the earth. This observation is formulated by Ambassador Niccolini to Urban VIII in the actual terms of the argument which had been put forward by the Pope: if we cannot say that the heliocentric system is the only way in which God could create the universe, we cannot on the other hand even state that it was the only way in which He could not have created it; the demonstration of the heliocentric theory is admitted, therefore, on the level of de facto truth: «[...] but that there is an argument to which they have never been able to reply, which is that God is omnipotent and can do any thing; if He is omnipotent, why do wew wish to subject Him to necessity? I said that I did not know how to speak about this matter, but that it was my opinion that I have heard it said by this same Signor Galilei, first that he did not hold the opinion of the movement of the earth as true, but that if God could make the world in a thousand different ways, then we cannot deny that He could have made it in this way", Ed. Naz., XV, p. 68. G. DE SANTILLANA, *Processo a Galileo*, op. cit., pp. 321-326, dates the discussion to 1624, on the occasion of the audience granted by Urban VIII to Galileo, in the corse of which the problem of the value of the arguments in favour of the Copernican system was certainly resumed and discussed as a mere hypothesis, on the basis of what had already been said on the occasion of the discussion of 1616. For a closer analysis of the argument of Urban VIII from the epistemological viewpoint, see G. MORPURGO TAGLIABUE, *I processi di Galileo e l'epistemologia*, op. cit., pp. 99-107.

[89] Ed. Naz., X, p. 350, see also P. PASCHINI, *Vita*, op. cit., pp. 192-195.

[90] Ed. Naz., V, p. 102.

[91] Ed. Naz., V, pp. 297-298. W. R. SHEA, *La rivoluzione intellettuale di Galileo*, op. cit., pp. 122-123, observes that: «An undoubted conflict is revealed in Galileo's mind between the certainty which he claims for geometric demonstrations and the awareness of the hypothetical character of his own speculations». It should be remembered that for Galileo, the hypothesis is not a fiction, but a conjecture which is awaiting to be proved false or true; the conclusions, therefore, are not probable but certain.

[92] Ed. Naz., V, pp. 377-395.

[93] Ed. Naz., XII, p. 242.

[94] Ed. Naz., XIX, pp. 322-323. The episode of Maffeo Barberini's intervention to prevent the Copernican thesis being declared heretical is mentioned by Giovanfrancesco Buonamici: «[…] whence, Paul V, instigated by these same friars, without the opposition and defence of the Lord Cardinal Maffeo Barberini and of the Lord Cardinal Bonifatio Gaetano, would have declared this Copernican system erroneous and heretical, as contrary to the teaching of Scripture in certain places and in particular in Joshua: but the said Lords Cardinal, thus for the reputation of Nicholas Copernicus, who since he had been the principal master of the reform of the year could not, without the mockery of the heretics who do not accept this reform, be declared heretical in a position which was in any case purely natural […]», Ed. Naz., XIX, pp. 408-409; also by Campanella in his comment on the *Adulatio perniciosa*, written by Barberini to exalt the astronomic findings of the scientist; see S. PIERALISI, *Urbano VIII e Galileo Galilei,* op. cit., pp. 25-26; T. CAMPANELLA, *Lettere*, edited by V. Spampanato, Bari 1927, pp. 221-225; and also by the biographer of Urban

VIII, Mons. HERRERA, *Memorie intorno alla vita di PP Urbano cavate dall'originale di Mons. Herrera al quale S. Santità le dettava,* Biblioteca Apostolica Vaticana, cod. Barb. Lat, 4901, fol. 40r-v: «Urbano, while he was still cardinal in the Pontificate of Paul V, when the matter arose of prohibiting the work of Nicholas Copernicus because of his opinion about the motion of the earth, was of the opinion that it should not be prohibited but that the things that seemed necessary should be corrected in his writings, because in the remaining part it was useful, and Gregory XIII had made use of it in the correction of the calendar. This was followed up and proved to be successful. The same judgment was given by Cardinal Gaetano, and Ballarmine, after consulting with the geometricians, approved it greatly».

95 Ed. Naz., XIX, pp. 400-401. The stages of the «emendation» of the *De revolutionibus* are documented by the Decrees of the Sacred Congregation of the Index of 2nd April, 3rd July, 7th September 1618, 28th February 1619, 31st January 1620. From the Decrees we learn that in the meeting of 2nd April, presided over by Bellarmine, a speech was made by Ingoli, in which after the importance and necessity for astronomers to make use of the *De revolutionibus* was recognised, the criteria to be followed for the revision of the text were given. The Congregation decided to refer the speech of Ingoli to the mathematicians of the Collegio Romano for an opinion. In the meeting of 3rd July it was noted that the book of Copernicus and the speech of Ingoli had been examined by the mathematicians of the Collegio Romano and that Cristofer Grienberger and Orazio Grassi had approved the proposal of Ingoli that all astronomers should be allowed to make use of the *De revolutionibus.* In the meeting of 7th September a deliberation was taken concerning the «epistle» which had featured as an introduction to the new and revised edition of the *De revolutionibus.* On 28th February 1619, the Congregation, on the basis of a report by Francesco Ingoli, decided to include the *Epitome astronomiae Copernicanae* of Kepler which had been published in 1618 in the list of prohibited books. Finally, in the meeting of the Congregation on 31st January 1620, the publication of the «corrected» edition of *De revolutionibus* was decided. It should be noted that Maffeo Barberini participated in the meetings of 7th September 1618, February 28th 1619 and 31st January 1620: a further and significant testimony of the interest in the Copernicus-Galileo question and the role which he played in it: his action was supported by Ingoli – who took on himself the paternity, and thus the responsibility, of limiting the condemnation of the *De revolutionibus* to a correction of certain statements by Copernicus – and by the two authoritative mathematicians of the Collegio Romano, Grienberger and Grassi. For the text of the Decrees see *Copernico,*

Galileo e la Chiesa. Fine della controversia (1820). Gli atti del Sant'Ufficio,
a cura di W. Brandmüller and E. J. Greipl, Florence 1992, pp. 148-149.

96   Ed. Naz., XIX, pp. 321-322. The two propositions subjected to
examination by the Qualificators were not drawn either from the works of
Copernicus or from those of Galileo, but were formulated on the basis of the
depositions of Caccini, in an imprecise and often obscure fashion. See A.
BANFI, *Vita del Galileo Galilei*, Milan 1962, pp. 157-158; G. DE
SANTILLANA, *Processo a Galileo*, op.cit., pp.288-291: «Sol est centrum
mundi et ideo immobilis motu locali. Terra non est centrum mundi nec
immobilis, sed secundum se totam movetur etiam motu diurno». Probably
Caccini and the qualificators, as has been mentioned (see note 57) used the
same astronomical text, *La sfera del mondo*, by A. Piccolomini. On 24th
February 1616, the Qualificator Theologians, eleven in all, declared the first
proposition ridiculous and absurd in philosophy and formally heretical, and
formulated an identical censure for the second, which as far as the faith was
concerned was to be regarded as «at least erroneous». On the following day
Cardinal Mellini notified the censure to the Commissary and to the
Assessors of the Holy Office, and communicated to Bellarmine the order of
Paul V «ut vocet coram se dictum Galileum, eumque moneat ad deserandam
dictam opinionem; et si recusavit parere, P. Commissarius, coram notario et
testibus faciat illi praeceptum ut omnino abstineat huiusmodi doctrinam et
opinionem docere aut defendere, seu de ea tractare; si vero non acquieverit,
carceretur». On 26th February the censures were communicated by
Bellarmine to Galileo: then followed the admonition and the precept
according to the written report in Cart. 378v-379r of the Vatican Codex.

97   The publication of the records of the trial raised the question of the
authenticity of the precept and its juridical value. The problem was raised
by E. WOHLWILL, *Der Inquistionprocess des Galileo Galilei. Eine
Prüfung seiner rechtlichen Grundlage nach den Akten der römischen
Inquisition*, Berlin 1870, and taken up subsequently by all who were
interested in the trial of the scientist. The authenticity of the document
written in the same hand and the same ink as the preceding minute, was
then upheld by F. H. REUSCH: *Der Process Galilei's und die Jesuiten*,
Bonn 1879, and by H. GRISAR, *Galileistudien Historischtheologische
Untersuchungen über die Urteile der römischen Congregationem im
Galilei Process*, Regensburg, New York and Cincinnati 1882. K. VON
GEBLER, in *Galileo Galilei e la Curia romana*, op. cit., II, pp. 36-46, also
does not accept the theory of a forgery; he holds the annotation to be
authentic but of no juridical value. In the search for the original document
of the precept, he applied, through the mediation of the Austrian

ambassador to the Holy See, to the Secretary of State, Cardinal Giovanni Simeoni, to ask him to research in the Archives of the Holy Office to find the original document of the precept. The search produced no result, according to what the Cardinal wrote to the historian, pp. 44-45. E. COSTANZI, *La Chiesa e la dottrina copernicana*, op. cit., pp. 320-325. D. BERTI, in *Copernico e le vicende del sistema copernicano in Italia nella seconda metà del secolo XVI e nella prima metà del secolo XVII*, Rome 1875, pp. 245-250, believes that the deed attesting the precept is authentic and was formulated by the Commissary and transcribed at a later time by the notary: in this way the absence of Galileo's signature and that of the Notary and witnesses is explained. This theory was accepted by O. GIACCHI, *Considerazioni giuridiche sui due processi contro Galileo*, in *Nel terzo centenario della morte di Galileo*, op. cit., p. 383: «On this now ancient and surpassed question the objective observations of D. BERTI seem to me still useful from the juridical point of view». But despite the opinion of the eminent canon lawyer, it does not seem to me that the observation can be considered to be «surpassed»; given the special juridical nature of the precept, as an act which brings into being an absolute ban, from which, in the case of violation, the gravest spiritual, disciplinary and penal consequences may arise, the formality of the written reaction, on the spot and with the signature of the person concerned as well as the notary and witnesses, must be required for its official status and legal validity: in fact, therefore, it is a matter, in my view, of a legally null and void document. What leaves us with many doubts about the effective injunction of the precept is that this deed alone, of such importance, which concluded the proceedings initiated against Galileo, remains without signatures, when all the records of the interrogations and depositions are signed with the formula: «Quibus habitis etc. fuit dimissus, imposito sibi silentio cum iuramento de praedictis et obtenta eius subscriptione». It should also be added that the precept was notified only if the person who was warned had not promised obedience to the exhortation which was addressed to him in it; but on more than one occasion, Galileo had declared that he submitted himself to the ecclesiastical authorities. In this context we should remember the conclusion of the *Discorso sul flusso del mare*, delivered to Cardinal Orsini, in which he defends the Copernican theory: «And finally for a last conclusion and seal of this my short Discourse, if the hypothesis assumed, and corroborated only by philosophical and astronomical reasonings, should declared, by virtue of more pre-eminent knowledge, to be false and erroneous, it would be appropriate not only to call in question this writing of mine but to consider it totally vain and out of the question [...]», Ed.

Naz., V, p. 395. There was thus no reason not to accept the admonition and to open a dispute on the matter with Bellarmine and with the Commission of the Holy Office. G. DE SANTILLANA, *Processo a Galileo*, op. cit., pp. 269-283, after a careful examination of the written notations on the document and the way in which the pages on which the written acts of the trial were bound in the Codex, has shown that the precept which we possess is a mere transcription of a document which cannot be found among the papers of the process. In fact «it is very likely that it was never drawn up in the original, and that it appears solely under the form of a transcription which cannot pretend to be anything more than a copy». Santillana repeated this judgment; see *Nuove ipotesi sul processo a Galileo* in *Saggi su Galileo Galilei*, op. cit., pp. 474-486. J. BRODRICK, *Robert Bellarmin*, op. cit., on the other hand opts firmly for the theory of a forgery, p. 307: «[...] the document of 26th February 1616 is nothing but a forgery, drawn up by an unknown person who wanted to deliver Galileo to the Inquisition in the event that he went on upholding the reality of the Copernican system». For an effective summary of the problems raised by this precept, see also A. KOESTLER, *I sonnambuli*, op. cit., pp. 456-458. Finally the explanation of the precept proposed by S. DRAKE, *Galileo at work. His scientific biography*, Chicago and London 1978, pp. 253-254, is appealing but does not, I think, find backing in the documents.

98 Ed. Naz., XIX, p. 278 on the summoning of Galileo by Bellarmine , see V. CAPPELLETTI, *Il dramma di Galileo,* in *La scienza tra storia e società,* Rome 1978, pp. 363-364.

99 Ed. Naz., XII, p. 248.

100 Ed. Naz., XIX, p. 348. The handwritten copy of the letter has been published in *The Louvain Lectures (Lectiones Lovanienses),* op. cit., p. 25.

101 Ed. Naz., XIX, pp. 390-391.

102 Ed. Naz., XII, pp. 422-423.

103 Ed. Naz., XII, p. 428.

104 Ed. Naz., VI, p. 41.

105 *De tribus cometis anni MDCXVIII. Disputatio astronomica publice habita in Collegio Romano Societatis Jesu ab uno ex patribus eiusdem societatis,* Romae 1619, Ed. Naz., VI, pp. 23-25. On the question of the comets and the subsequent polemic between Galileo and Fr Orazio Grassi, see W. R. SHEA, *La rivoluzione intellettuale di Galileo,* op. cit., pp. 102-141.

106 Ed. Naz., XII, p. 443.

[107] *Discorso delle comete di* MARIO GUIDUCCI *fatto da lui nell'Accademia Fiorentina nel suo medesimo consolato,* Florence 1619, Ed. Naz., VI, pp. 39-105; see also A. FAVARO, *Amici e corrispondenti,* op. cit., III, pp. 1413-1474.

[108] Ed. Naz., VI, *Discorso delle comete,* pp. 46, 48, 73-74, 88-89, 92-93.

[109] Ed. Naz., XII, p. 466; see also W. BRANDMÜLLER, *Galilei e la Chiesa ossia il diritto di errare,* Città del Vaticano 1992, pp. 83-87.

[110] *Libra astronomica ac philosophica qua Galilaei Galilaei opiniones de Cometis a Mario Guiducio in Florentina Academia expositae, atque in lucem nuper editae, examinantur a Lothario SARSIO Sigensano,* Perusiae 1619, Ed. Naz., VI, pp. 111-179.

[111] Ed. Naz., XII, p. 499.

[112] Ed. Naz., XIII, p. 23.

[113] W. R. SHEA, *La rivoluzione intellettuale di Galileo,* op. cit., pp. 118-119.

[114] In the *Discorso* of Mario Guiducci, Galileo had not missed the opportunity to stress how important for the solution of the problem of the comets it was to have a sound knowledge of the system of the universe, with a semi-concealed reference to the Copernican conception. «Seneca knew, and wrote, how important for the sure determination of these things it was to have a firm and indisputable knowledge of the order, disposition, states and movements of the parts of the universe, of which our century remains devoid: however, it behoves us to be content with that little which we can conjecture, thus amid the shadows, until the true constitution of the parts of the world is attained, since that which was promised us by Tycho remains imperfect», Ed. Naz., VI, pp. 98-99. Grassi naturally had not failed to reply to Galileo's observation, which was aimed at stressing the lack of trustworthiness of Tycho's system, with a clear reference to the condemnation of the Copernican thesis: «Quem potius sequeretur? Ptolemaeum? Cuius sectatorum iugulis Mars, proprior iam factus, gladio exerto imminet? Copernicum? at qui pius est revocabit omnes ab illo potius, et damnatam nuper hypothesim damnabit pariter et reiiciet. Unus igitur ex omnibus Tycho supererat, quem nobis ignotas inter astrorum vias ducem adscisceremus. Cur igitur Magistro meo ipse succenseat, qui ullum non aspernatur? Frustra hic Senecam invocat Galilaeus, frustra hic luget nostri temporis calamitatem, quod vera ac certa mundanarum partium dispositio non teneatur, frustra saeculi huius deplorat infortunium, si nil habeat quo hanc ipsam aetatem, hoc saltem nomine eius suffragio miseram, fortunet magis», Ed. Naz., VI, p. 116 .

115 Ed. Naz., VI, p. 233. Galileo was careful to correct a judgment of Grassi concerning the Copernican system, naturally with due caution: «And in conclusion, if the movement attributed to the Earth, which I as a devout and Catholic person, consider very false and null, should be adapted to give explanation of so many and so varied appearances which can be observed in the heavenly bodied [...]», and he again puts forward the argument which he had already advanced in the *Discorso* on the tides, to demonstrate the movement of the earth.

116 MAFFAEI Card. BARBERINI *nunc* URBANI VIII *Pont. Max.*, *Poemata*, Perusiae 1628, pp. 52-55.

117 Ed. Naz., VI, p. 201.

118 Ed. Naz., XIII, pp. 141, 146. On G. Ciampoli v. D. CIAMPOLI, *Nuovi studi letterari e bibliografici*, Rocca S. Casciano 1900, pp. 5-170; A. FAVARO, *Amici e corrispondenti di Galileo,* op. cit., I, pp. 135-189; M. COSTANZO, *Critica e poetica del primo Seicento*, I. *Inediti di Giovanni Ciampoli (1590-1643),* Rome 1969; A. DE FERRARI, *Giovanni Ciampoli,* in *Dizionario Biografico degli Italiani,* Rome 1981, pp. 147-152; M. GUGLIELMINETTI – M. MASOERO, *Lettere e prose inedite (o parzialmente edite) di Giovanni Ciampoli,* in «Studi Secenteschi», XIX (1978), pp. 131-237; M. TORRINI, *Giovanni Ciampoli filosofo* in *Novità celesti e crisi del sapere,* op. cit., pp. 267-275.

119 Ed. Naz., XIII, pp. 146-147.

120 Ed. Naz., XIII, p. 182.

121 Niccolò Riccardi, born in Genoa in 1585, entered the Dominican Order during his stay in Spain: Philip III nicknamed him Padre Mostro because of his eloquence, his memory and his gigantic stature: in 1623 he had read and approved the *Saggiatore* with the ecclesiastical reviser, with expressions of great praise: «[...] I do not believe that our century will glory in its inheritance solely because of the efforts of the philosophical passages, but also because of the discoverer of many secrets of nature that the philosophers could not discover, the fruits of the subtle and sound speculations of the author, in whose time I repeat I am content to have been born, when the gold of truth is measured no longer by the scales and the weight, but with such delicate essays». Nominated as Master of the Sacred Palace in 1629, he took a leading role in the publication of the *Dialogo* and the trial. Despite the severe provisions threatened against the ecclesiastical revisers who had granted the permission to print the *Dialogo*, he was not removed from his office, a point of some importance for maintaining that

Riccardi had in fact obtained the permission to print the Dialogue from Urban VIII. He died on 1st may 1639. See I. TAURISANO, *Series Chronologica Magistrorum Sacri Palatii Apostolici ab anno 1217 ad annum 1916*, in *Hierarchia Ordinis Praedicatorum*, Rome 1916, p. 56.

122 Ed. Naz., XIII, p. 181. On the German humanist Gaspare Scoppio and his action in favour of Galileo, see M. D'ADDIO, *Il pensiero politico di Gaspare Scioppio e il Machiavellismo del Seicento,* Milan 1962, pp. 173-175.

123 Ed. Naz., XIII, p. 182: «[...] As for the things for which I have mainly received great honours and favours from Our Lord the Pope, having been as many as six times in lengthy discussion with him [...]. Among the other Lords Cardinal, I have been many times with great enjoyment in particular with Santa Susanna, Buoncompagno and Zollern, who left yesterday for Germany, and told me that he had spoken with His Holiness on the matter of Copernicus and how the heretics are all of his opinion, and take it for a certainty, and that nevertheless one must be very circumspect in coming to any conclusion; to which it was replied by His Holiness, that Holy Church had not condemned and was not about to condemn it as heretical, but only as audacious, but that it was not to be feared that anyone was about to demonstrate that it was true of necessity. Father Mostro and Signor Scioppio, although they are far from being able to enter as much as would be needed into such astronomical speculations nevertheless hold very firmly the opinion that this is not a matter of faith, and nor does it in any way impugn the Scriptures».

124 It should be pointed out that the conviction of Urban VIII that the tides did not provide a proof of the movement of the earth around the sun had found confirmation in that year in the work (dedicated to his nephew Cardinal Francesco Barberini) by Marcantonio De Dominis, *Euripus,* in which it was maintained that the tides were due to lunar attraction. V. E. DE MAS, *Il «De radiis visus et lucis». Un trattato scientifico pubblicato a Venezia dallo stesso editore del «Sidereus nuncius»,* in *Novità celesti e crisi del sapere,* op. cit., pp. 165-166.

125 Ed. Naz., VI, pp. 509-561. In the conclusion of the *Letter,* Galileo referred to the scheme of the *Dialogo dei massimi sistemi:* «This is what I have to say to you for now in response to your physical and astronomical objections against the system of Nicholas Copernicus: this argument could be treated in a much wider way, if the time and strength is granted to me to bring to an end my Discorso on the flow and ebb of the tide, which, taking as its hypothesis the movements attributed to the Earth, gives me as a consequence a wide field to examine at length all that has been written on this matter».

126   Ed. Naz., VI, pp. 510-511; see, with regard to the further examination of the hypothetical concepì on the part of Galileo in the *Letter to Ingoli,* G. MORPURGO TAGLIABUE, *I processi di Galileo e l'epistemologia,* op. cit., pp. 78-85.

127   Ed. Naz., XIII, p. 295.

128   Ed. Naz., XIII, p. 265. «I was many times with my lord the prince of Sant'Angelo (Federico Cesi) discussing you and your works, both those completed and those still to do. On the advice of His Excellency, I delayed sending to Ingoli the letter written to him, and I will continue to defer it for as long as Your Holiness, despite the considerations of my Lord the prince, does not order the contrary. The considerations are as follows: First that a few months ago, in the Congregation of the Holy Office, it was proposed by a reverend person that the *Saggiatore* should be prohibited or corrected, with the imputation that the doctrinbe of Copernicus concerning the movement of the earth is praised in it. About this matter a Cardinal assumed the task of informing himself and reporting on the case; and by great good fortune he decided to give the responsibility to Fr Guevara, General of a kind of Theatine Order who, I believe are called the Minimi. This Father then went to France with my Lord Cardinal Legate. He read the work diligently and as he seemed quite pleased with it, he praised it and recommended it highly to that same Cardinal, and also wrote down certain defences, in which that doctrine of movement, when it was also held, did not seem to him to be fit for condemnation. And thus things were quietened down for that period". The episode, recorded by Galileo, according to a recent work by E. REDONDI, *Galileo eretico,* Turin 1983, pp. 173-219, did not concern the accusation that the Copernican thesis was upheld by the *Saggiatore,* given that the proposal of the «anima pia» in effect was nothing other than the anonymous denunciation, at present preserved in the Archive of the Sacred Congregation for the Doctrine of the Faith, and rediscovered by Redondi, in which it was stated that the theories of Galileo concerning heat were contrary to Eucharistic doctrine (pp. 427-429). The denunciation must have been presented by Fr Orazio Grassi, who in his *Ratio ponderum librae et simbellae* published in Paris in 1626 in response to the *Saggiatore* obseved that the theory of Galileo concerning heat, by reducing the real qualities of matter to a sensible perception of the subject, ended by denying the Eucharistic doctrine of trans-substantiation. Guevara, according to Redondi, drew up an opinion on this point, maintaining the compatibility of the Galìleian notion with Eucharistic doctrine: Guiducci, not well informed, must have fuddled the matter by confusing the movement of corpuscles and atoms, from which heat is derived, with the movement of the earth. The

denunciation, set aside in 1625, was to be taken up again and re-presented to Galileo by Grassi and other mathematicians of the Collegio Romano on the occasion of the publication of the *Dialogo dei massimi sistemi* (March-July 1632), and thus it may have constituted the real reason for the trial of Galileo, who was, in contrast, to be accused of having upheld the Copernican thesis, only because this latter was far less serious than the former, and thus to avoid some truly dramatic consequences (pp. 294-340). It should immediately be said that this interpretation of the trial of 1633 does not find any support or correspondence in the documents concerning Galileo which would serve to uphold it, as indeed the author himself acknowledges (pp. 306-307). We may observe, concerning the "anonymous denunciation" published by Redondi, that this document, drawn up in the customary chancery script of the first thirty years of the seventeenth century, is not formulated as a «denunciation», but rather as an «opinion», almost certainly addressed to the Master of the Sacred Palace, written, therefore, by one of the assessors of the Congregation for the Index for the occasion of the granting of the *Imprimatur* for the printing of the *Saggiatore* It should be noted that the information of Guiducci on the episode is very precise and does not leave room for doubt: he had obtained it from Federico Cesi, who had numerous friends among the College of Cardinals, and hence in the Congregation for the Index and the Holy Office. The favourable report of Guevara was almost certainly founded on the statement that the thesis of heliocentricity could be sustained and illustrated *ex hypothesi* as we can see from the decree of the Congregation of the Index itself, and as Fr Grassi himself held, from what Guiducci tells us: "End here we fell to discussing the movement of the earth, of which Your Worship made use *ex hypothesi* and not as a principle established as the truth: at which the Father said, that when it was a matter of demonstration of this movement, which involved interpreting the Holy Scriptures otherwise than had been done in the places where the issue was the stability of the earth or the movement of the heavens, and this *by the sentence of Cardinal Bellarmine,* to whose opinion he completely gave his assent" Ed. Naz., XIII, p. 203. It should also be noted that Guevara had had an opportunity to meet Galileo in Florence, and to discuss with him various problems his studies related to a comment, later published, on the *Mechanics* of the School of Aristotle. It is extremely unlikely that he would not have informed Galileo of the episode to which Guiducci referred; if there had been discussion about the contrast between the theory of heat and the Eucharistic doctrine the scientist would almost certain have taken note of it, if for no other reason than to defend himself, in the notes which he attached to the *Ratio ponderum librae et simbellae*. In fact, in these latter notes instead of limiting himself to noting – with a touch of mischief – that the *Saggiatore* had been published with the approval of the Church, while the *Ratio* had appeared without the prescribed permits from the Superiors Ed. Naz., VI, p. 486. For further considerations, reference should be made to my article, *Alcune fasi dell'istruttoria del processo a Galileo,* in «L'Osservatore Roman», 2-3-1984; for a broad critical examination of the theory of Redondi, see V. FERRONE - M. FIRPO, *Galileo tra inquisitori e micro-storici,* in «Rivista storica italiana», 1985, pp. 177-238.

129 Ed. Naz., XIV, pp. 87-88.

130 T. CAMPANELLA, *Opere letterarie*, edited by L. Bolzoni, Turin 1977, pp. 678-680: «Sic Sancti Dominicus et Franciscus et Bernardus, novas regulas vivendi in Christianesimo condentes, non sunt novatores, sed potius confirmatores et instauratores caritatis, fidei, spei, humilitatis et dogmatum, quae Apostoli praedicavere. Sicut enim coruscante Evangelio, ut ait Hieronimus, nova interpraetatio scripturis sacris debebatur, ita et rerum naturae tum et Evangelio, tum et detecto per Columbum orbe novo et novis per Galileum stellis, nova debetur interpretatio".

131 S. PIERALISI, *Urbano VIII e Galileo Galilei*, op. cit., pp. 25-27, Campanella agreed basically with the thesis upheld by Urban VIII, and was convinced of the, so to speak, «provisional» character of scientific knowledge, but at the same time, he recognised the scientific validity, even though contingent and not absolute, of Galileo's discoveries; on this point see G. MORPURGO TAGLIABUE, *I processi di Galileo e l'epistemologia*, op. cit., p. 117.

132 T. CAMPANELLA, *Lettere,* op. cit., pp. 223-224: «And then in No. 8 I did not say that Your Beatitude might be in favour of the opinion of Copernicus, but since it is written in the new Index, if I remember rightly, by order of Your Beatitude, that one may hold his book to be a *hypothesis*, when he says that the earth moves, adding this condition, that if it were to move it would follow... etc., *et conditionalis non ponit in esse* by the rule of logic I have not implied that Your Beatitude might favour this opinion, but that *"sustinendum hypothetice cum philosophorum commodo et reipublicae incolumitate simul mira providentia curavit"*. For in fact it was necessary to hold to Copernicus, because the reform of the Calendar gives true and powerful testimony of his observations, but not of his opinions, and because it serves quite well for the astronomers, and with the expression: *"hypothetice* it may be held" he forestalls Your Beatitude to the Church and the scientists, and removes the error, and this was what I

praised, as can be well seen in the first and eighth number. But if I have not explained myself well, and it could be improved, command me how it should be done».

[133] Ed. Naz., XIII, p. 365.

[134] Ed. Naz., XIV, pp. 77-78.

[135] Ed. Naz., XIV, p. 78.

[136] Ed. Naz., XIV, p. 83.

[137] Ed. Naz., XIV, p. 103.

[138] Ed. Naz., XIV, p. 11.

[139] Ed. Naz., XIV, p. 113.

[140] Ed. Naz., XIV, p. 120.

[141] Ed. Naz., XIV, p. 121.

[142] Ed. Naz., XIV, p. 254.

[143] Ed. Naz., XIX, p. 330: previously, on 24th May, Riccardi had indicated to the Inquisitor at Florence the conditions to which the permit to print was subject: the letter specified, very significantly: «… to be the mind of Our Lord (the Pope)…». Ed. Naz., XIV, p. 327. On the events concerning the publication of the *Dialogo* see P. PASCHINI, *Vita*, op. cit., pp. 477-489.

[144] Ed. Naz., XIV, p. 331.

[145] Ed. Naz., XV, p. 25.

[146] Ed. Naz., XIX, p. 410. On Buonamici and his reports on the Galileo trial, see A. FAVARO, *Amici e Corrispondenti,* op. cit., I, pp. 104-121. Also, Luca Holstein, in a letter from Rome dated March 1633, pointed to Maculano as one of those responsible for the initiative for the trial, Ed. Naz., XV, p. 62.

[147] Ed. Naz., XIV, p. 339.

[148] Cf. *ibid.*; M. CIONI, *I documenti Galileiani del S. Ufficio di Firenze*, Florence 1908, no. XVI, p. 23.

[149] Ed. Naz., XIV, p. 346.

[150] Ed. Naz., XIV, p. 351.

[151] Ed. Naz., XIV, p. 357-358.

[152] Ed. Naz., XIV, p. 366.

153 Ed. Naz., XIV, p. 360. Galileo's Roman friends, and naturally the scientist himself, were convinced that the mathematicians of the Collegio Romano would have had a decisive part in raising the incompatibility of the *Dialogo* with the decree of 1616, and in bringing the case before the Holy Ofice. This was the sentiment that Galileo himself expressed in a letter to Diodati in July 1634, a year after the condemnation: «They have finally wished to show themselves to me, given that a dear friend of mine was in Rome for about two months, discussing with Fr Cristoforo Gremberger, a Jesuit and mathematician of that College; when matters concerning me were raised, the Jesuit said these formal words to my friend: "If Galileo had been able to retain the affections of the fathers of this College, he would be living gloriously in the world and there would have been none of his disgrace, and he would have been able to write according to his judgment on any matter, I mean also the movement of the earth and so on. Certainly your lordship will be aware that it is not this not that opinion that has brought war upon me and still does, but the fact of being in disgrace with the Jesuits"». Ed. Naz., XVI, p. 117, F. FLORA, *Il processo di Galileo*, op. cit., pp. 100-101. Undoubtedly the polemic aroused by the question of the comets had provoked animosities, suspicion and resentment on both sides, and in the end an academic dispute, which was directed at a purely scientific question, was presented as a religious issue. However, within the context of the Collegio Romano, there were discussions and differences of opinion on the attitude that should be taken to the issue of Galileo: this is attested by Fr Grassi himself (see note 82). The evidence preserved in Galileo's correspondence agrees in identifying Fr Scheiner as the promoter of the initiative aimed at subjecting the *Dialogo* and its author to the judgment of the Holy Office. He was a long-time adversary of Galileo, since the time of the polemic over the priority of the discovery of sunspots. In the *Dialogo* Galileo had criticised the Scheiner's *Disquisitiones* and his *Rosa ursina* – not without some polemical attacks – naturally causing a strong reaction in the latter, wo at once showed his determination to draw up a response to the *Dialogo*, which he was to publish much later on, the *Prodromus pro sole mobili et terra stabili contra Academicum Florentinum Galilaeum a Galilaeis*. In February 1633, he also communicated to Gassendi his intention to conunter the theses of the *Dialogo:* «Prodierunt nuper 4 Galilei Dialogi italice conscripti, pro motu terrae Copernicano stabiliendo conscripti contra communem Peripateticorum scholam [....]. Quid tibi videtur de his? Multis non placet ista scriptio. Ego pro me et veritatis defensionem paro [...]». In July he informed Kirker of the conclusion of his *Prodromus* and of the condemnation of Galileo, Ed. Naz.,

XV, pp. 47, 184. Scheiner must have been particularly zealous in Roman ecclesiastical circles in maintaining «his truth», so much so as to lead Gabriel Naudé to hold that it was in the Jesuit mathematician that the «promoter» of the trial must be identified; he wrote of it to Gassendi in April 1633: «[...] for the Court of Rome, where Galileo has been cited by the actions of Fr Scheiner and other Jesuits, who want to make him lose [...]», and then to Nicola Peiresc: «[...] M. Naudé wrote to me that Fr Scheiner wrote from then onwards *ex professo* against poor Galileo, that he worked powerfully and with very great animosity [...]»; this was confirmed too by Gaffarel in May of the same year: «He will know this sad news of poor Galileo, that he has been imprisoned by the Inquisition. Fr Scheiner, a Jesuit, is the one who has organised this, *ut creditur...*», Ed Naz., XV, pp. 88, 164, 141. After the condemnation, Mattia Bernegger, the translator of the *Dialogo* into Latin, once again accused Scheiner: «Et ne ante carcerem scriptas existimes istum squallorem et persecutionem illam (quae potissimum a Scheiner, Jesuita quodam, auctore et instinctore profiscitur) patienter a se ferri ostendit [...]. Videris tibi Socratem quondam in carcere coincionantem audire», Ed. Naz., XVII, p. 365.

154 M. CIONI, *I documenti Galileiani*, op. cit., p. 24.

155 Ed. Naz., XIV, pp. 369-370.

156 Ed. Naz., XIV, p. 371.

157 Ed. Naz., XIV, p. 372.

158 Ed. Naz., XIV, p. 373.

159 Ed. Naz., XIV, pp. 375-376.

160 Ed. Naz., XIV, p. 377.

161 Ed. Naz., XIV, pp. 379-381.

162 Ed. Naz., XIV, p. 382

163 Ed. Naz., XIV, pp. 383-384. The denunciation to the Holy Office, as regards the *Dialogo* and its author, was taken up after the work and conclusions of an appropriate Congregation, of which Urban VIII gave notice to Niccolini. According to Redondi (*Galileo eretico*) this was a case of an extraordinary procedure to get Galileo out of the very serious accusation of having expounded and upheld a theory, that concerning heat, which was contrary to Eucharistic doctrine, and to «fall back on» the other, far less grave one, of having violated the decree of 1616 (pp. 309-325). The sources of which we know do not offer any support or confirmation to validate such a supposition. In effect the Congregation was rendered

necessary by the simple fact that the *Dialogo* had been approved by the Master of the Sacred Palace, and by the Inquisitor of Florence, and it was known in the Curial circles that the Pope had been informed of the publication. A prior examination of the book is necessary, therefore, in order to establish whether or not it initiated the inquistorial process. The «limited commission» which prepared the work of the Congregation was made up of Riccardi, the Jesuit mathematician Inchofer, and the Papal theologian, Agostino Oreggi. Riccardi, who kept first Filippo Magalotti and then Niccolini informed on the work of the Congregation, despite the rule of secrecy, would certainly have referred to the question, if for no other reason than to demonstrate the effort made in defence of Galileo and to exempt himself from responsibility for the events that were taking place. Campanella, who followed the work of the Congregation from close quarters, to such an extent that he was able to get one Cardinal to intervene on Galileo's behalf, would also have had news of this and would have found a way of informing the scientist of it.

164 Ed. Naz., XIV, p. 385.

165 *Ibid.*

166 Ed. Naz., XIV, p. 388-389.

167 Ed. Naz., XIV, p. 392.

168 Ed. Naz., XIX, pp. 279-280.

169 Ed. Naz., XIV, p. 397. On Campanella's intervention see F. FLORA, *Il processo di Galileo,* op. cit., pp. 122-123.

170 Ed. Naz., XIX, p. 634.

171 On the «character Simplicius» and Urban VIII, see E. COSTANZI, *La Chiesa,* op. cit., pp. 273-281; K. V. GEBLER, *Galileo Galilei e la Curia romana,* op. cit., I, p. 214; A. FAVARO, *Oppositori di Galileo X. Maffeo Barberini,* in «Atti R.I.V. di scienze, lettere e arti», 1920-21, t. 80, p.te 2°, pp. 26-29; G. DE SANTILLANA, *Processo a Galileo,* op. cit., pp. 347-351, who speaks of «a tactical error by Galileo» and observes that «it is amazing that neither he nor his allies had realised it»; A. BANFI, *Vita di Galileo Galilei,* op. cit., pp. 234-235; P. PASCHINI, *Vita,* op. cit., pp. 605-607. About a year and a half after the sentence, Castelli sought to undo the «calumny» of the identification of Simplicius with the Pope, speaking of this to Cardinal Antonio Barberini, the Pope's brother and a member of the Court of the Inquisition which had judged Galileo: «[...] and that which urges me on a good deal is that I have begun to try to persuade the Most Eminent Lord Cardinal Antonio (and he has shown that the thing is dear to

him) that the calumny laid upon your most illustrious self, that in your Dialogo you meant to indicate by Simplicius that person who is worthy of the highest of all honour; I have, I repeat, urged upon his Eminence in the way of truth that this calumny is utterly false, and he has told me that he wishes to speak when the occasion arises to those who are necessary in order to obtain all good offices», Ed. Naz., XVI, p. 363. Very probably as a result of this intervention, Urban VIII declared to the ambassador of France, François de Noailles, that he had intervened in favour of Galileo, and that he had understood that the scientist did not intend to refer to him by Simplicius, but that he remained troubled by the fact that adequate explanation of his thesis had not been given, Ed. Naz., XVI, p. 450.

172 On the episode of the conflict between Spain, the Empire and Urban VIII, in which the protagonists on the Spanish side were the Borgias, and on the Imperial side, Pázmány, see L. VON PASTOR, *Storia dei Papi dalla fine del Medioevo*, XIII, Rome 1943, pp. 435-457; and more specifically A. LEMAN, *Urbain VIII et la rivalité de la France et de la Maison d'Autriche de 1631 à 1635*, Lille-Paris 1919.

173 The Viceroy of Naples, in order to support the motives and position of the Borgias, had threatened the calling of a Council, and intervention, if necessary, by the force of arms; a firm initiative on the part of the Emperor had been backed by Pázmány on his return to Austria, and the idea of a General Council figures among the opinions that were presented to Philip IV by theologians who had been asked to judge the question. See L.VON PASTOR, *Storia*, op. cit., XIII, pp. 444, 457. On the importance of the episode for the purposes of the trial of Galileo, see F. GREGOROVIUS, *Urbano VIII e la sua opposizione alla Spagna e all'Imperatore*, Rome 1879, p. 107; A.BANFI, *Vita di Galileo Galilei*, op. cit., pp. 236-238, which notes among the items of news left by a contemporary: «He suspects that the apparatus created at Naples is aimed at him, that the fleet of the Grand Duke of Tuscany is ready to sail towards Ostia and Civitavecchia, thus he is reinforcing their garrisons»; G. MORPURGO TAGLIABUE, *I processi di Galileo e l'epistemologia*, op. cit., pp. 120-125.

174 On the relations between Ciampoli and Urban VIII, following the clamorous initiative taken by Cardinal Borgia, and on his expulsion from the Roman Curia, see A. FAVARO, *Amici e corrispondenti di Galileo*, op. cit., I, pp. 166-171, which makes use, in relation to this episode, of the despatches of Ambassador Niccolini to Florence; on the initiative of Borgia, the letter from Niccolini dated 11th March is particularly interesting (pp. 120-122); on 25th April Niccolini wrote: «Among so many other

things, Mons. Ciampoli, as an esteemed friend ... has completely fallen from grace«; between 25th August and 25th September, he informed his correspondent that «he has had orders to leave the Palace, and it has been made known to Mons. Ciampoli that he must content himself with taking any Government that he may find». The political misfortunes of Ciampoli had decidedly negative repercussions on the *Dialogo*, which in those very months was beginning to circulate in Roman ecclesiastical circles. Urban VIII returned more than once, on the occasion of an audience granted to Niccolini, to the relation between Ciampoli and Galileo, blaming the prelate for the initiative taken to print , and accusing him of being the main person responsible for the «deception» of which he had been a victim, including the Master of the Sacred Palace and the Inquisitor of Florence: «Then he went on to tell me that in short he had been ill-advised to utter these opinions of his abroad, and that it was a certain "Ciampolata" that this was done [....]»; «[...] may God help Ciampoli some time with these new opinions, because he too has a whiff of them, and is a friend of the new philosophy», Ed. Naz., XV, pp. 56,68.

175 Ed. Naz., XIV, p. 383: «I replied that Sig. Galilei had not gone ahead and printed without the approval of these ministers, and that I myself had obtained and ordered the prefaces for this purpose. He replied with the same fury that he and Ciampoli had deceived him, and that Ciampoli in particular had gone so far as to say that Sig. Galileo had sought to do everything that his Holiness commanded, and that all was well, and that this was what he knew without ever having seen or read the work; complaining about Ciampoli and the Master of the Sacred Palace, although he says that it was by the latter that he was deceived [...]».

176 Ed. Naz., XIV, p. 254: «P. Stefani will have judiciously reviewed the book but not knowing the feelings of our Lord, cannot give approval that it is enough fo me to give it, so that the book may be printed without some dismay on his and my part, if they then find something in it which discords with the prescriptive orders [...] and this I cannot do by the permission to print alone, because this does not fall to me, but only by assuring that it is in conformity with the rule that has been given him by order of our Lord the Pope».

177 Ed. Naz., XIX, p. 327. Riccardi also specified that Galileo's work must deal [...] «absolutely with the mathematical consideration of the Copernican position concerning the movement of the earth, with the aim of proving that, when the revelation of God and sacred doctrine was removed, appearances could be saved in that position by dissolving all the contrary

persuasions that might be deduced from experience and from peripatetic philosophy, so that absolute truth could not, certainly, be conceded to that opinion, but only the hypothetical truth, and without the Scriptures. It is still to be shown that this work is made only to show that there are all the necessary reasons which can be adduced for this part, and that it is not for lacking of knowledge of them that this sentence has been passed in Rome, conforming to the principle and the purpose of the book which from here on will be adjusted». These indications are «scrupulously» taken up by Galileo and carried in the introduction which the scientist made sure was included in the text of the *Dialogo* as a warning of the hypothetical nature of the Copernican system.

178 Ed. Naz., XIV, p. 384.

179 Ed. Naz., XIX, p. 410. The witness of Buonamici seems, if only indirectly, to be borne out by the fact that according to what Niccolini says, Riccardi, in the investigatory stage of the trial declared that he did not feel any concern as regards the revision and the subsequent licence to print of the *Dialogo:* «[…] unless I should speak of it to the Master of the Palace, who says that it is very well defended as regards what is presupposed about the revisions and printing licences for the book […]», Ed. Naz., XIV, p. 377. It should also be remembered that Buonamici was well-informed on the precedents of the Galileo affair (see the pages of his *Diary* in Ed. Naz., XV, p. 111), and above all well-placed in the ecclesiastical surroundings of the Congregation of the Sacred Office. In fact he succeeded, once the trial was over, to have a copy of the sentence, while Guiducci, who had been appealed to by Galileo for one, could not obtain it, because of the particular procedure by which the sentence must have been made public, Ed. Naz., XV, p. 241.

180 Ed. Naz., XIV, pp. 406-410.

181 Ed. Naz., XIV, pp. 428-429.

182 Ed. Naz., XIV, pp. 401-402.

183 Ed. Naz., XIV, pp. 387-388.

184 Ed. Naz., XV, p. 273.

185 Ed. Naz., XIX, pp. 326-327.

186 Ed. Naz., XIX, pp. 281-282; *I Documenti,* op. cit., p. 108.

187 Ed. Naz., XV, p. 51.

188 Ed. Naz., XV, p. 71.

189 Ed. Naz., XV, pp. 67-68.

190 Ed. Naz., XV, p. 45.

191 Ed. Naz., XV, p. 56.

192 Ed. Naz., XV, pp. 103-104.

193 Ed. Naz., XIX, p. 339; *I documenti*, op. cit., p. 126.

194 Ed. Naz., XIX, p. 340.

195 Ed. Naz., XIX, p. 339 (117-8); *I documenti*, op. cit., p. 127.

196 Ed. Naz., XV, pp. 106-107; E. COSTANZI, *La Chiesa e le dottrine copernicane*, op. cit., pp. 318-320, shows how the letter from Maculano registers the perplexities which had emerged in the course of the trial over the whole matter: «In every line of this document [...] there can be observed a certain anxiety, and the desire to avoid going too far with the trial; in it there is also an allusion to a certain basis, adopted by Maculano, in favour of an extra-judicial solution of the case, to difficulties, to consequences which it seems he does not dare to formulate or expound, but which tell us that all does not appear clear and transparent in this affair, and how the officials of the Court and even the Prosecutor in the trial, were affected by doubts and hesitancies».

197 Ed. Naz., XIX, p. 341 (194-195); *I documenti*, op. cit., p. 131.

198 Ed. Naz., XV, pp. 106-107. On the intervention of Maculano and the «confession» of Galileo, see G. MORPURGO TAGLIABUE, *I processi di Galileo e l'epistemologia*, op. cit., pp. 135-143.

199 On the profound convictions of Galileo about the ultimate purpose of his activities as a scientist, which brought him close to Campanella, we should take note of the just onclusions of R. AMERTO, *Galileo e Campanella: la tentazione del pensiero nella filosofia della Riforma cattolica,* op. cit., p. 302: «Belonging to the Church is, for Galileo and Campanella, the indispensable condition for their life, their honour and their philosophising. Not only this: it is the paradoxical condition for thinking which makes it possible to overcome the temptation of thought. This silent intransigeance concerning the membership of the church, and the substantial claim of the orthodox character of the new truths bring the teaching of these two thinkers so close that it is justifiable to see in it one of the main trends of that century, and a truly progressive assertion of the philosophy of Christianity».

200 Ed. Naz., XV, p. 45.

201 Ed. Naz., XV, p. 85.

202 With regard to the declaration by Galileo concerning the *Dialogo* and the subsequent memorandum in its defence presented on 10th May to accompany the letter issued to him by Bellarmine in May 1616, see Ed. Naz., XIX, pp. 342-348.

203 Ed. Naz., XIX, pp. 345-347; *I documenti*, op. cit., pp. 135-136.

204 Ed. Naz., XV, pp. 109-110.

205 Ed. Naz., XV, p. 132.

206 Ed. Naz., XIX, pp. 282-283; *I documenti*, op. cit., p. 229.

207 Ed. Naz., XV, p. 160.

208 Ed. Naz., XIX, p. 361.

209 Ed. Naz., XIX, p. 362; *I documenti*, op. cit., p. 155. On the occasion of the publication of the acts of the trial, the question was raised and examined relating to the torture to which Galileo was alleged to have been subjected. The sentence in fact reads: «And since it seems to us that he had not told the truth entirely about your intention, we judged that it was necessary to take action against you by rigorous examination, in which, without, however, any prejudice to the things confessed by you and deduced against you as above concerning your said intention». On the basis of this passage of the sentence, Jagemann maintains, specifically, that Galileo was subjected to torture. L'Epinois, Gebler, Favaro, Giacchi, Paschini, Santillana have all denied that he was tortured. Recently, S. MEREU, *Storia dell'intolleranza in Europa*, Milan 1979, pp. 397-414, has newly maintained the claim of torture, with a detailed examination of the sentence and of the abjuration – in his judgment the only «certain» documents – on the basis of the procedure followed by the courts of the Inquisition. But as G. MORPURGO TAGLIABUE rightly observed in *I processi di Galileo e l'epistemologia*, op. cit., pp. 198-199: «No interpreter has ever shown it (to be true) and no text from the process documents it». In fact the information that we possess on the stages of the trial and what we can glean from the Niccolini correspondence preclude the allegation of torture; it should be noted above all that it was not the practice of the Inquisition to subject elderly persons to torture; Galileo was seventy years old and moreover was suffering, as we know, from a hernia. If he had been subjected to torture between 23rd and 29th April, Niccolini, who had obtained permission to visit the prisoner every evening, would surely have become aware of it, and would have written to the Grand Duke, and in any case would have referred to the matter on the occasion of Galileo's return to

the ambassador's residence in the Villa Medici. Nor can the claim that Galileo was subjected to torture on 21st June be upheld, when the "rigorous examination" was actually carried out as had been ordered in the previous meeting of the Congregation of the Holy Office, presided over by Urban VIII (in the course of which torture was threatened for the one and only time), both because the written report makes no mention of it and states that the scientist's replies had been considered sufficient to asacertain his "true intention", and because it is hard to believe that Galileo, if he had been tortured, would have had the strength to go the day after to the convent of Santa Maria sopra Minerva, to protest his catholic faith, hear on his knees the sentence, and pronounce his abjuration. Buonamici, who was in Rome in those days, and was so fiercely polemical towards Urban VIII and Maculano, would certainly not have failed to stigmatise the latest injury and torment inflicted on his friend.

[210] Ed. Naz., XV, p. 164: see also the letters of Niccolini and Bouchard, XV, pp. 165-166.

[211] Ed. Naz., XIX, pp. 402-406.

[212] Various authors have pointed out the lack of the three signatures in the subscription of the sentence: K VON GEBLER, *Galileo Galilei e la Curia romana*, op. cit., I, pp. 315-317; S. PIERALISI, *Urbano VIII e Galileo Galilei*, op. cit., pp. 218-220; A. FAVARO, *Intorno ad un episodio non ancora chiarito del processo di Galileo*, Venice 1902; G. DE SANTILLANA, *Processo a Galileo*, op. cit., pp. 567-568.

[213] Ed. Naz., XIX, p. 283.

[214] Ed. Naz., XV, p. 160.

[215] On this point, and on the "faults in form" which affect the whole procedure followed in regard to Galileo, see V. CAPPELLETTI, *Il dramma di Galileo*, op. cit., p. 366.

[216] G. DE SANTILLANA, *Processo a Galileo*, op. cit., pp. 567-568.

[217] Ed. Naz., XV, p. 25.

[218] Ed. Naz., XIX, p. 393.

[219] U. BALDINI, *L'astronomia del Cardinal Bellarmino,* in *Novità e crisi del sapere,* op. cit., p. 305.

[220] L. FROIDMONT, *Anti-Aristarchus, sive Orbis Terrae immobilis liber unicus, in quo decretum S. Congregationis S.R.E. cardinal. an. 1616 adversus Pythagorico-Copernicanos editum defenditur*, Antwerp, 1631, p. 97.

221 On the reaction of Descartes to the sentence, see Ed. Naz., XV, pp. 340-341, p. 56. The letters in which Descartes expresses reservations about the sentence are, in particular, those of February and April 1634, addressed to Mersenne: «And moreover, since it has not yet been seen that either the Pope or the Council has ratified that prohibition, made only by the Congregation of Cardinals established for the censorship of books, I would be very relieved to hear what is maintained now in France, and whether their authority was sufficient to make it an article of faith». This reservation was taken up again in a subsequent letter, not without a touch of malice: the sentence might have suffered the same fate as the declaration of heresy concerning the Antipodes: «[…] so that, since it is not yet clear that this censure has been authorised by the Pope, nor by the Council, but only by a special congregation of Cardinal Inquisitors, I do not indeed lose hope that it will meet the same fate as the Antipodes, which they had in much the same way condemned previously […]»; again in March 1641, he returned to the matter of the condemnation, to criticise strongly the mixture of Aristotelianism and the Bible: «[…] those who mix Aristotle with the Bible, and seek to abuse the authority of the Church in order to exercise their passions – I mean those who have caused Galileo to be condemned, and who would much like to condemn my own opinions also, if they could, in the same way; but if that ever comes into dispute, I shall make every effort to show that there is no opinion, in their philosophy, which accords so well with the faith as my own». See *Oeuvres de Descartes*, pub. by CH. ADAM & P. TANNERY, *Corrrespondance*, Paris 1897-99, t. I, pp. 281,288, t. III, pp. 349-350. On the relations between Descartes and Galileo, see C. FERRO, *Galileo e Cartesio*, in *Nel terzo centenario della morte di Galileo Galilei*, op. cit., pp. 327-350. It should be noted that Mersenne had, in the *Quaestiones ad Genesim*, Paris 1623, cols. 879-890, returned to the belief of St Augustine, maintaining that the Copernican question did not come into the context of the doctrine of faith; on the relations between Mersenne and Galileo, see R. LENOBLE, *Mersenne ou la naissance du mécanisme*, Paris 1943, pp. 391-413. With reference to the judgment of Gassendi on the sentence, see *De motu impresso a motore translato*, Ch. II, t. III, p. 519. On Mersenne, Gassendi and Pascal and the Copernico-Galileian system see P. ROSSI, *Aspetti della rivoluzione scientifica*, op. cit., pp. 154-157. For an assessment of the judgments of Descartes, Mersenne and Gassendi on the sentence, see E. COSTANZI, *La Chiesa e le dottrine copernicane*, op. cit., pp. 335-339; L. GARZEND, *L'Inquistion et l'hérésie. Distinction de l'hérésie théologique et l'hérésie inquisitoriale: a propos de l'affaire Galilée*, Paris 1912, pp. 465-471; A. BEAULIEU, *Les réactions des savants*

français au début du XVII° siècle devant l'heliocentrisme de Galilée, in *Novità celesti e crisi di sapere,* op. cit., pp. 373-381.

222 G. B. RICCIOLI, *Almagestum Novum,* Bononiae 1651, t .I, par. II, p. 486; his judgment on the sentence takes account of the observations of Gassendi and of the Jesuit H. Fabri against recognising in the sentence the declaration of a principle of faith in favour of the geocentric system, and also of the considerations of Lipsius, Inchofer and Polacco, which on the contrary favoured retaining the Ptolemaic conception of faith. In defence of Galileo's theories as upheld in the *Dialogo,* there was an intervention by Fr STEFANO DEGLI ANGELI, *Considerazioni sopra la forza di alcune ragioni fisio-matematiche addotte dal M.R.P. Gio. Battista Riccioli Ges. nel suo Alamgesto nuovo e Astronomia riformata contro il sistema Copernicano espresse in due Dialoghi,* Venice 1667. For the polemic, see J. J. E. DREYER, *Storia dell'aastronomia da Talete a Keplero,* Milan 1970, pp. 383-390; for an assessment of the judgment of Riccioli on the sentence, see M. VIGANÒ, *Il mancato dialogo fra Galileo e i teologi,* op. cit., pp. 230-233; P. PASCHINI, *Vita,* op. cit., pp. 592-593.

223 EUSTACHIUS DE DIVINIS (pseudonym of H. FABRI), *Pro sua annotatione in systema Saturnium Christiani Hugegnii adversus eiusdem assertionem,* Romae 1661, p. 49.

224 A. FAVARO, *Sulla pubblicazione della sentenza contro Galileo e sopra taluni tentativi del Viviani di far revocare la condanna dei Dialoghi galileiani,* op. cit., p. 143.

225 A. MÜLLER, *Niccolò Copernico,* op. cit., p. 179. On the actions taken by Leibniz in favour of the Galileo question during his journey in Italy, see V. FERRONE, *Scienza natura religione. Mondo newtoniano e cultura italiana nel primo Settecento.* Naples 1982, pp. 40-46.

226 A. A. KOCHANSKI, *Considerationes et observationes Physico-Mathematicae circa diurnam Telluris vertiginem a multis absque certis Demonstrationibus assertam quarum aliquot Methodi proponuntur,* in «Acta eruditorum», Leipzig 1685, pp. 317-327; on Kochanski and the Galileian school see M. TORRINI, *Dopo Galileo, Una polemica scientifica* (1684-1711) Florence 1979, pp. 57-62; it should also be remembered that another Jesuit mathematician had defended Galileo in 1680, in a writing published anonymously: see M. TORRINI, *G. Ferroni, gesuita e galileano,* «Physis», 1973, pp. 411-423.

227 On the Galileo tradition in the late seventeenth and early eighteenth centuries in Italy, see A. PAOLI, *La scuola di Galileo nella storia della*

filosofia, in «Annali delle Università toscane», XXII, 1899, p. IICCCVII; *La Scuola Galileiana. Prospettive di ricerca*, in *Atti del convegno di studi di Santa Margherita Ligure (26-28 ottobre 1978)*, Florence 1979; U. BALDINI, *La scuola galileiana*, in *Storia d'Italia*, Annali, III, Turin 1980, pp. 383-463; especially interesting for the role that the issue of Galileo played in the cultural renewal promoted by the group of «enlightened» Catholics V. FERRONE, *Scienza, natura religione*, op. cit., pp. 3-168.

228 L. FERRARIS, *Biblioteca canonica, giuridica, moralis, teologica... in octo tomos distributa*, Rome 1759, t. III, pp. 336-337; in the notes reference is made to a decree of the Holy Office of 1712, of which there is no trace in the sources; this is almost certainly a material error, since the only possible reference is to the decree of the Congregation of the Index of 1620: «Hac de causa vetitum est hanc opinionem tueri velut thesim; nam ut hypothesis propugnari et doceri potest ex Decreto Supremae Inquisitionis anni 1712. Imo si in eo Philosophi devenirent, ut evidenti demonstratione ostenderent, quiescere Solem in centro mundi, ac terram moveri, statim permitteretur omnibus hanc opinionem amplecti; sicuti universim tenemus dari antipodas contra plures Patres, qui exponentes secundum litteram non nullos Scripturae textus dari antipodas inficiati sunt. Hoc in casu diceremus, Scripturam de solis motu loquentem, non vero qua ratione motus illi juxta natuae leges fiant». On Ferraris' *Bibliotheca canonica* see W. BRANDMÜLLER, *Commento*, in *Copernico, Galilei e la Chiesa*, op. cit., pp. 38-40.

229 On the Padua edition of Galileo's Works, see A. FAVARO, *Galileo Galilei e lo studio di Padova*, Florence 1883, II, pp. 439-441; V. FERRONE, *Scienza natura religione*, op. cit., pp. 136-138.

230 Ed. Naz., XIX, p. 419. The decision by Benedict XIV not to include on the Index the books that upheld the heliocentric thesis also corresponded to the wish expressed in the fourth volume of D'Alembert's *Encyclopédie* (1754). He was the author of the entry «Copernicus» in which, after having recorded in summary form the proofs of the Copernican system, the events of Galileo's condemnation, and the reasons adopted, at the time, to resolve the conflict with Scripture, noted that this system was universally accepted in France and England: «It would be much to hope that a country as full os spirit and knowledge as Italy should finally wish to to recognise an error so prejudicial to the progress of science, and that they should think rather of this matter as we do in France! Such a change would be truly worthy of the enlightened pontiff who governs the Church today; a friend of science and a man of learning himself, it is for him to give the law to the inquisitors on

this subject, as he already has on other matters of importance». D'Alembert pointed out, with an indirect reference to St Augustine and St Thomas, the appropriateness of recognising that Revelation had faith as its object, not the knowledge of nature, to avoid that erroneous statements, given backing b y the Scriptures, however, should have a negative effect on religious convictions: «This fury of the Inquisition about the movement of the earth even does harm to religion: in effect what will the weak and the simple think of the real dogmas that the faith obliges us to believe, if it is found that mingled with these dogmas there are doubtful or false opinions? Would it not be better to say that Scripture, in matters of faith, speaks according to the Holy Spirit, and in matters of physics must speak like the people, whose language it was necessary to use in order to bring itself within their reach?», *Encyclopédie ou Dictionnaire raisonné des Sciences, des Arts et des Métiers,* ed. an., Stuttgart-Bad Cannstatt 1966, IV, pp. 173-175; see also W. BRANDMÜLLER, *Commento,* in *Copernico, Galilei e la Chiesa,* op. cit., pp. 35-36.

231 *Astronomie,* par M. DE LA LANDE, 2nd edition, t. I, Paris 1771. The astronomer undertakes a critical examination of the objections to the Copernican system (pp. 529-536), to conclude: «Moreover, we should regard as direct and positive demonstrations of the movement of the earth [...] the phenomenon of the abberration of stars [...] the flattened figure of the earth [...] the shortening of the pendulum towards the equator, and all the phenomena which prove the general attraction of celestial bodies [...] because this law would not be able to exist without the movement of the earth, which is the first basis of all astronomy and all celestial physics». He deals later with the exegetical question of the passages of Scripture (pp. 536-541), and appealing among others to St Augustine, S. Thomas, Campanella, and Kepler, maintains the possibility of interpreting the biblical passages in the light of the Copernican notion: «The natural conclusion of all the foregoing is that the Copernican system is the only one which can be admitted: it is proven, as far as any physical thing can be».

232 *Ibid.,* p. 539.

233 *Ibid.,* p. 540.

234 L. BRENNA, *De vita et scriptis Galilei Galilaei,* in A. FABRONI, *Vitae Italorum doctrina excellentium, qui saeculis XVII et XVIII floruerunt,* Pisa 1779, I, pp. 133-134.

235 G. TIRABOSCHI, *Storia della letteratura italiana,* Milan 1833, IV, *Memoria storica prima. Sui primi promotori del sistema copernicano.* Delivered in the Accademia dei Dissonanti on 15th March 1792, pp. 502-506;

Memoria storica seconda. Sulla condanna di Galileo e del sistema copernicano. Delivered in the same Academy on 7th March 1793, pp. 506-511.

236   *Ibid.*, p. 509: «But it is still true that he makes this interlocutor Simplicius, to whom he entrusts the part of defending the old system, utter such simplicities, and support his opinion so weakly, that some people suspected that Galileo, under the name of this Simplicius, sought to cast a shadow over and deride some of his censors, and there were even those who suspected, although in my opinion with less reason, that Pope Urban VIII was intended to be designated by that name».

237   G.TIRABOSCHI, S*ui primi promotori del sistema copernicano*, op.cit., p. 502.

238   G. TIRABOSCHI, *Sulla condanna del Galileo e del sistema copernicano*, op. cit., pp. 510-511.

239   G. TIRABOSCHI, *Storia della letteratura italiana*, op. cit., IV, p. 443.

240   *Ibid.*, p. 438. On Tiraboschi and the Dominican Tommaso Mamachi, the Master of the Sacred Palace who expressed reservations about certain judgments which appeared in the *Memorie storiche*, see W. BRANDMÜLLER, *Commento*, in *Copernico, Galilei e la Chiesa*, op. cit., pp. 41-44.

241   In the Archive of the Sacred Congregation for the Doctrine of the Faith, the file relating to the publication of the *Elementi di ottica e di astronomia* by Canon Giuseppe Settele is preserved (Stanza Storica E.5.b), which aroused a controversy over competent authority as regards the granting of the *Imprimatur,* between the Congregation of the Holy Office and the Master of the Sacred Palace, Filippo Anfossi. The documents relating to this "controversy" were collected, at the care of the Holy Office itself, in a «stampato» (publication) possessed by the Vatican Apostolic Library (R. G. Miscell. 251 [2]); *Suprema Sacra Congregazione del S. Ufficio. Sopra uno scritto stampato rimesso alla S.C. da Sua Santità fattole presentare dal R.P. Filippo Anfossi, Maestro del Sacro Palazzo Apostolico contro la dottrina della mobilità della terra e dichiarazione degli antichi Decreti nelle Ferie IV 16-23 agosto 1820. Ristretto di ragione e di fatto con sommario di documenti e di allegazioni*, November 1820. The most important reports and documents on the question are noted, among them the full report by Fr Maurizio Benedetto Olivieri, Commissioner of the Holy Office (favourable to the granting of the imprimatur and to the decision that the Copernican theory should be proposed as a «thesis» and no longer as a «hypothesis»), and the two opinions of Mons. Anfossi:

Ragioni per cui il P. Maestro del S. Palazzo Apostolico ha creduto e crede che non si può permettere la stampa del manoscritto del sig. canonico Settele, pp. 2-13; *Supplica presentata in marzo p.p. a S.Santità dal Professore Settele*, pp. 13-20; *Riflessioni di Fra Maurizio Benedetto Olivieri*, pp. 21-83; *Voto del Rev.mo P. Consultore D. Antonio Maria Grandi Pro-Vicario Generale dei Barnabiti, ordinatogli con decreto della Suprema Sacra Congregazione nella Rer. IV 9 agosto p.p.*, pp. 89-92; *Motivi per cui il P. Maestro del S. Palazzo Apostolico ha creduto e crede non doversi permettere al Signor Canonico Settele di insegnare come tesi e non come semplice ipotesi a tenore del Decreto del 1620, la mobilità della Terra e la stabilità del Sole nel Centro del Mondo*. After the death of Fr Olivieri an essay of his was published, dedicated specifically to the Galileo issue, and in it he takes up again the report which had been presented to the Holy Office: *Di Copernico e di Galileo scritto postumo del Padre Maurizio Benedetto Olivieri, ex generale dei Domenicani e Commissario dell S. Rom. ed Univ. Inquisizione, ora per la prima volta messo in luce sull'autografo per mezzo di un religioso dello stesso Istituto*, Bologna 1872. The whole file relating to the question raised by the Master of the Sacred Palace, Anfossi, has recently been published with a substantial introductory commentary, which makes it possible to reconstruct the precedents for the decision of the Holy Office of 16th August 1820: see W. BRANDMÜLLER, *Commento*, in *Copernico, Galilei e la Chiesa*, op. cit., pp. 15-130; E. J. GREIPL, *Introduzione, ibid.*, pp. 133-141, *Documenti*, pp. 143-484.

242 Ed. Naz., XIX, p. 420. The objections and resistance put up by the Master of the Sacred Palace did not prevail; they resulted in an attempt to defend the informative spirit of the trial of 1633; a new and accurate examination and the relative discussions lasted two years, but at the end of these, in its meeting of 11th September 1822, the Congregation of the Holy Office, after having renewed the vote made in 1820, provided as follows for matters concerning any future resistance to the new deliberation: «[...] reluctantes et inobedientes praevia quatenus opus sit, derogatione praetensorum privilegiorum, coercendos esse poenis arbitrio S. Congregationis»; on 25th September, Pius VII approved the decree of the Congregation, Ed. Naz., XIX, p. 421. On the whole affair, see W. BRANDMÜLLER, *Commento*, in *Copernico, Galilei e la Chiesa*, op. cit., pp. 161-192.

243 The opinion of Galileo scholars on the strictly disciplinary value of the sentence of 23rd June 1633 is virtually unanimous: it referred exclusively to the personal question of Galileo posed by the publication of the *Dialogo*, did not set out any principle of faith, and should not have been

interpreted as an absolute ban on studying the Copernican theory from a scientific viewpoint, even though it could not be taught as the «true» astronomic theory. V. L. GARZEND, *L'Inquisition et l'hérésie*, op. cit., pp. 480-484; E. VACANDARD, *Galilée*, in *Dictionnaire de la Théologie Catholique*, VI (I) Paris 1920, cols. 1082-1083; M. VIGANÒ, *Il mancato colloquio tra Galileo e i teologi*, op. cit., pp. 229-231; F. SOCCORSI, *Il processo di Galilei*, op. cit., pp. 52-54; G. DE SANTILLANA, *Processo a Galileo*, op. cit., pp. 580-583. The fact that the sentence should have a purely disciplinary content, and that it was not founded on any principle of faith, has posed a further problem, as regards the imposition of the solemn abjuration, which presupposes the violation, or the suspicion that there has been a violation, of a principle of faith fomally declared. Abbot D. BONIX, *La condamnation de Galilée, Lapsus des écrivains qui l'opponuit à la doctrine de l'infaillibilité du Pape*, in «Revue des sciences ecclesiastiques», Paris, Feb-Mar. 1866, holds that this was certainly a matter of «an arbitrary (sentence) and an injustice», caused not by «ill will» but by an «error»; K. VON GEBLER, *Galileo Galilei e la Curia Romana*, op. cit., I, p. 314, stresses the illegitimacy from the canonical point of view of the solemn abjuration: «The spiritual Court had indeed the right to punish the disobedience of the learned man with spiritual chastisement and with prison, and to prohibit him in disciplinary terms from discussing that opinion in word or in writing; but it was not in any way authorised to demand from Galileo or from anyone else the taking of such a profession of faith about a doctrine which had not been defined by any infallible authority». E. COSTANZI, *La Chiesa e le dottrine copernicane*, op. cit., pp. 373-374: «But from the doctrinal point of view, and according to Canon Law, the judges went too far and forced the interpretation of the Sacred text, by involving the Faith in the Copernican issue, and describing the doctrine of the stability of the Sun and the movement of the Earth as heretical, and also by obliging Galileo not only to recant and to withdraw, but to pronounce a formula of abjuration». V. CAPPELLETTI, *Il dramma di Galilei*, op. cit., p. 364.

[244] R. AMERIO, *Galileo e Campanella: la tentazione del pensiero nella filosofia della Riforma cattolica*, op. cit., pp. 299-302.

[245] Ed. Naz., XIX, p. 411. On Galileo's abjuration, see A. C. JEMOLO, *Meditando sul processo di Galilei*, in *Saggi su Galileo Galilei*, op. cit., pp. 504-506. P. SIMONCELLI, *Storia di una censura*, op. cit., p. 124, stresses particularly the correction by Lamalle in the text of Paschini: «abiura letta», corrected to «abiura detta»: the first expression implies a merely passive attitude on the part of Galileo; the second, on the other hand an actual

acceptance; he then makes it clear that the author of this essay must have followed the censorious interpretation of Lamalle. This observation does not correspond in any way to what is maintained at the conclusion of the essay: we suggest a careful reading of the note, in which it is stated that the abjuration was an unjust imposition, according to what the authors mentioned had already observed; it is then noted that the concluding judgment of the essay refers to the testimony of Buonamici, according to which Galileo, after the essential reservations at the abjuration – which was thus an act of mere passive obedience – *read* the formula which had been prepared. It should be noted in fact that what Buonamici reports corresponds precisely with what Galileo himself wrote to Niccolò Fabri, in December 1635: «[…] two comforting things aid me perpetually; the one is that in the reading of all my works there will be no one who can find the merest shadow of anything which detracts from piety and reverence for the Holy Church; the other is my own conscience, fully consulted by myself alone on earth, and in Heaven by God, which well understands that in the cause for which I suffer, many may have done so far more learnedly, but none of the Sacred Fathers even, could have been able to proceed and speak more piously nor with greater zeal towards the Holy Church, nor indeed with holier intenstions than I have», Ed. Naz., XVI, p. 215.

INDEX OF NAMES

FABER G., *78, 85.*
FABRI H. (LEFÈVRE, DE DIVINIS), *149, 201.*
FABRI N., *207.*
FABRIS R., *169.*
FABRONI A., *153, 203.*
FAILLA P. I., *172.*
FARNESE O., CARD., *29, 51.*
FAVARO A., *7, 16, 142, 159-160, 164, 166, 177, 184-185, 190, 193-194, 198-199, 201-202.*
FEMIANO S., *171.*
FERRARIS L., *150, 202.*
FERRO C., *200.*
FERRONE V., *189, 201-202.*
FERRONI G., *201.*
FIRPO L., *160, 171.*
FIRPO M., *189.*
FLORA F., *167, 191, 193.*
FONTONE S., *46.*
FOSCARINI P. A., *42, 46-47, 54-55, 67, 128, 171, 175-176.*
FROIDMONT L., *146-148, 199.*

GAFFAREL G., *192.*
GAINO T., *161.*
GALAMINI A., CARD., *38.*
GALATI D., *160.*
GALLANZONI G., *30.*
GALLUZZI P., *159, 162, 164, 175.*
GARRONE G. M., CARD., *.8, 9.*
GARZEND L., *200, 206.*
GASSENDI P., *148, 191-192, 200-201.*
GEBLER F. V., *160, 181, 193, 198-199, 206.*
GEMELLI A., *16, 160, 162.*
GESSI B., CARD., *138, 142.*
GHERARDI S., *160.*
GHERARDINI N., *111-112.*
GHISLIERI F., *37.*
GIACCHI O., *182, 198.*
GIACOMETTI G., *161.*
GIESE T., *20, 22, 24, 161.*

GINETTI M., CARD., *118, 138, 142.*
GONZAGA L. ST, *170.*
GONZAGA V., CARD., *51.*
GRANDI A. M., *157, 205.*
GRASSI O. (SARSI L.), *73-80, 121-122, 180, 183-185, 187-188, 191.*
GREGORY XIII, *59, 89, 154, 170, 180.*
GREGORY XV, *44, 80.*
GREGOROVIUS F., *194.*
GREIPL E. J., *181, 205.*
GRIENBERGER C., *59, 121, 172, 176, 180.*
GRISAR H., *181.*
GUADAGNI M., *101.*
GUALDO P., *30.*
GUEVARA G. DE, *87, 120, 187-188.*
GUGLIELMINETTI M., *185.*
GUICCIARDINI P., *36, 66, 165.*
GUIDUCCI M., *75, 85-86, 102, 125, 184, 187-188, 196.*

HEATH D. D., *161.*
HERRERA F., *180.*
HOLSTEIN L., *190.*
HOSKIN M. A. E., *171.*
HUYGENS, *149.*

INCHOFER M., *147, 193, 201.*
INGOLI F., *60, 80, 84-86, 89, 136, 177, 180, 187.*
ISIDORO DI SIVIGLIA, *50.*

JAGEMANN CH. J., *198.*
JEMOLO A. C., *206.*
JOHN PAUL II, *8.*
JOUYEUSE F. DE, CARD., *29.*

KEPLER G., *16, 25, 27-29, 163, 165, 178, 180, 201, 203.*
KIRVITZER V., *172.*
KOCHANSKI A., *201.*
KOESTLER A., *161-163, 167, 175, 183.*